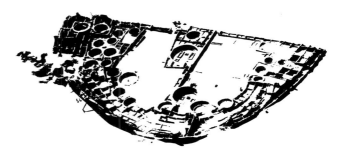

NATHANIEL ALEXANDER OWINGS **THE AMERICAN AESTHETIC**

PHOTOGRAPHS BY WILLIAM GARNETT

INTRODUCTION BY S. DILLON RIPLEY

HARPER & ROW, PUBLISHERS

NEW YORK, EVANSTON, AND LONDON

DESIGNER • JIM HILL

LIBRARY OF CONGRESS CATALOG CARD NUMBER: 68-28212

B-T

TO MY WIFE, MARGARET

ACKNOWLEDGMENTS

Although their names appear elsewhere in this book, I would like to say that without Bill Garnett's unfailing confidence in me and my message, this book would not have appeared; and that Jim Hill has done in the graphics what I have tried to do in the text, to make it a true expression of the American Aesthetic.

To John Macrae and Norbert Slepyan should go credit for being patient with a new author and for guiding him through the apparently endless maze of the publishing procedure; to Russell Butcher for his work on research for the historical sections; and to Marshall G. Sampsell, Peg Ireland and my wife for their inexorable demands for accuracy.

And lastly and most sincerely, my thanks to all of my partners in SOM for making it possible for me to do this book.

CONTENTS

INTRODUCTION

To be alive today somewhere between the college generation and the generation of the wholly retired and not to be skeptical and depressed about the way the world wags is difficult. Yet in this book Nathaniel Owings reveals clearly what those who know him have suspected—that he is perennially optimistic about the future. He is possessed of an unquenchable spirit of idealism about the potential of Americans and their land.

We Americans acknowledge the primacy of education. We continue to talk about the pursuit of happiness. And we couple these two themes, which tend to be somewhat mutually antagonistic, with the acceptance of the cardinal privileges of life and liberty.

However, education today has largely degenerated into training and the transmission of information. The accomplishment of the diploma, with its requisite skills, fails to equip anyone for the "pursuit of happiness." Our technocracy provides efficiency but not a safe, healthy environment for life itself. Certainly an educational system that produces human beings guaranteed to maintain our increasingly interconnected services seems to threaten subtly and indirectly perhaps our very freedom of choice.

Nathaniel Owings is right to emphasize that men wish to live functionally and relatively tidily and that they thus tend to create objects which serve their purposes well, and to embellish them, each according to his mode of expression, in charming and often beautiful flourishes. Some of us, as biologists, believe that certain higher animals also have an aesthetic sense. Experiments have demonstrated, for example, that some birds that develop duetting, or architecture, as the bower birds do, improve their creations when shown examples. This is important to remember in connection with contemporary art. At least among higher animals, training and example apparently are as fundamental in the development of an aesthetic sense as is skill.

Owings' keen eye and generous ways have endeared him to his fellow committeemen, like myself, who have had to think about the maintenance of a balance between "greenery and gallery" on Washington's Mall. My predecessor, the first Secretary of the Smithsonian, was fussing about this as far back as 1847 when he pleaded for the creation of Smithsonian Park, containing noble trees of native species, which he envisaged as potentially the pleasantest and most satisfying drive or walk anywhere in the nation.

Architects today find themselves in a dilemma of unprecedented proportions as many of their senior practitioners will testify. As Buckminster Fuller recently stated,*

*In "The Age of Astro-Architecture" by R. Buckminster Fuller, *Saturday Review*, July 13, 1968.

"The client who retains the architect tells him that he has already determined to produce a mortgage-bank prelogisticated building for a specific sum of money. The architect, 'has no real control,' no original design initiative, for he must design the kind of building the client already has in mind." As Owings says in this book, "name" architects are chosen for their individual trademark such as the grill or the arch, but ultimately the architect is usually a salesman who employs hordes of draftsmen to fit a startling shape over a piece of utilitarian space. The engineers, the bankers, the lawyers, and the real estate agents have already outwitted him, and the architect, an exterior decorator, can play with a few aesthetic decorations, limited choice of materials, windows, use of prefabricated modules, lobby lighting fixtures, and elevator car décor. This is about it.

Nevertheless, men like these have other things in mind. They urge us to use computer technology to improve living space. Technologies for doing so already exist, and the question is really not one of planning but one of accepting such technologies. We urgently need this acceptance, but how can we develop acceptance at all levels? Is the answer some form of total socialism extending government planning and control of the uses of land and natural resources so as to prevent individual control? Is the answer to remove the power of choice, limiting and if necessary closing the options to the landowner? Such a course rubs so against the American grain that it could be accomplished only by a revolution. Owings and architectural thinkers of like mind are opposed to such a course. They prefer to accomplish these objectives by voluntary means, such as an "urban coalition," perhaps composed of elements in the private sector of industry, working with government advice and approval. How, then, to gain acceptance for a topsy-turvy balance sheet, where short-term profits are subordinated to judicious long-term husbanding of natural resources to prevent blight, poverty, and physical and mental stress? Who will be the first to stop elbowing his way to the profits trough and to stop following the gravy train? Who will step aside and say, "I won't get in on the act, and I don't care what my stockholders think"?

Many young people are sufficiently disenchanted with the System that they can be mobilized to outvote the spoilers and to contribute talent and energy without concern for immediate profit. Spurred to cooperative action, students could embark on a crusade toward the common goal of creating vibrant cities, reforesting the rolling hills, cleansing our waters and estuaries. If this could be done, and if we can regard high-density urban areas merely as parts of space related to open space and think of our whole

nation as part of a mosaic of interlocking geophysical formations, each with its own special utility, then perhaps we can see dimly for the future the re-creation of the American Dream.

Among all the professions, I would urge the natural scientists to give special attention to these thoughts, for they are needed more than ever as part of the team. It is incumbent on biologists to believe in the possession by Americans of an aesthetic sense, however much the evidence of their eyes may aver to the contrary. For biologists must join with students of the social sciences and the arts in a common purpose, to create a study of what I have called "social biology," in which the true principles of ecology can be applied to social and urban studies of the city environment. Too often the pleas of city planners, architects, and designers go unheeded by the biologists. Still, nature, degraded, half-unrecognizable, is everywhere, and this vast old earth, traumatized by indignities and suppurating with decay as she lies endlessly violated by man, is still capable of being dealt with on fair and, we hope, healing terms. Let us, then, acknowledge that we possess an aesthetic sense.

S. DILLON RIPLEY

Flying over Chichén Itzá in the swampy jungles of Yucatan is like unrolling a stone-etched map. The Incas' terraced fields in the Andes are remnants of a world now gone. Similarly, patterns traced on the Mesopotamian landscape, temples along the Nile and the Great Wall of China circling and stretching into Mongolia are monuments to man's greatest hours. Civilizations leave marks on the earth by which they are known and judged. In large measure the nature of their immortality is gauged by how well their builders made peace with the environment.

In North America we may read our earliest history in the structures and ceremonial kivas left by the prehistoric pueblo builders on the floors of New Mexico's Chaco, Aztec and Bandelier Canyons, or clinging to the rock faces of Arizona's Canyon de Chelly, Betatian and Mesa Verde. Despite their isolation, these multistory clusters mark the strands of a giant web, each an organized society begun five or six thousand years before Christ; apart and yet connected, opening a window of fresh understanding.

Believing that the key to some of our present-day urban ills might be found imbedded in the imprints of these early cultures, photographer Bill Garnett and I made many flights over the great expanse of New Mexico, Arizona and Utah, over the mesas and juniper-studded earth, over the deep erosions of the canyon lands. What we saw confirmed my belief that the broad lessons to be gained from our past cultures can best be learned by interpretive study from the air.

What we saw was breathtaking. Rachel Carson's "long vistas of history" lay before us. Bewildering Monument Valley, with its ancient, massive forms, becomes a prophecy to be read from another chapter in time. Here, the slow-working tools of wind and water and the leaching of time have turned a wasteland into a wonder of towers and terraces, of thrusting forms and balancing masses, of color and texture. The Valley is a signature of a kind of beauty found nowhere but in America, and in this thrilling instant of recognition I could see in those towers and terraces great cities rising from the plains.

Could there be a prototype here for the broad forms of our cities and open spaces of the twenty-first century? The magnificence of this valley held something unique, offering a basis for a fresh American aesthetic, which in turn could inspire greater efforts in ways yet untried to develop cities that could support great populations and yet thrive in harmony with the surrounding land. Untried because unperceived, or because the idea was too enormous to comprehend. But whether or not we have the imagination to translate

14   Monument Valley, Navajo Tribal Park.

these lessons into guides for creating great cities, the fact remains that here lies the seed of a truly American aesthetic.

We have to clear the deck by admitting to the fallacies of our existing way of life. Only then can new sense of moral, spiritual and disciplinary control develop and be implemented through experimentation and exploration. In view of the strains exerted by population and technology, the outcome may well be the end of our society unless such controls are developed and the aesthetic fostered.

To define an aesthetic is an almost hopeless challenge. Involved are questions of individual and relative taste, flexible concepts of beauty and rigid principles of service. The more all-encompassing one tries to make his theory, the more elusive his goal seems to be. Whether the individual is creative and responsive or simply reaches out of the gray sea of mediocrity and says, "I like what I like," there is present an undeniable act of receptivity and judgment.

To each of us, the aesthetic has a special flavor. Those in covered wagons on the Santa Fe Trail saw it in the ever-lengthening vista to the West, devoid of men but eloquent of promise. A captain of industry may see in his head-office building the twentieth-century equivalent of the eleventh-century cathedral—raised, though, to the god of Profit and Loss. The conservationist looks to the dark stands of virgin redwoods for the aesthetic experience and for a spiritual sense of continuity. One doesn't use an aesthetic; one savors it as it comes to him. It can be self-perpetuating, and it is mellowed and enriched by time.

As a corollary to the need for the treatment of our physical surroundings as a totality, I am subordinating the aesthetic, as expressed by painting, sculpture, literature and the performing arts, to the whole environment.

Normally, one might think of our environment as consisting of two broad categories—all that the land and water and air encompass, including the complex relationships by which life is evolved and sustained, and that which is the result of man's actions. Yet man's activities have reached the point where nature and civilization have influenced each other so completely as to have established one system, one ecology, one total environment, from which come the conditions that govern our lives.

Primitive man could do little to change the broad world that surrounded him. Modern man has imposed the products of his system upon nature in the form of buildings, roads, pollutants. He has extinguished plant and animal species. He has altered nearly every facet of his surroundings. He cannot help but continue to do so—and in doing so, he will continue to alter himself. The question is not whether he *should* alter his environment, but whether he is going to alter it for good or for ill.

I have a conviction that whatever his other needs may be, man, in order to be happy, is compelled to express his love of beauty. Man's special need is to find and proclaim beauty in the manner in which he orders his surroundings. Thus, when we argue that the aesthetic sense separates the dignity of man from the mere functional existence of the termite, we may speak directly of accommodating his buildings to the land. Men and termites form societies of builders, but of all the known building creatures on this planet, only man seems to create beauty consciously in what he constructs. It is in service to this vital difference that this book has been written.

When I first discussed this search for "an American aesthetic" with my editor, he suggested that "if there is a traditional American aesthetic, it has evolved through commerce, not art."

This argument seemed to me an important point of departure, since it questioned the very existence of an American aesthetic, expressed concern over the propriety of the profit motive and the validity of an aesthetic developing out of "trade." If we cannot resolve these doubts and questions, then we will be chained to automation, over-specialization and a computerized society frighteningly soulless, like that of the white ant.

Nations, people and cultures develop their own peculiar aesthetic out of accidents of geography, time, events, endeavors and drives that express their ideas of themselves and their land. One need only note the differences between the exquisite intricacy of the buildings of the pre-Westernized China, the massive forms of ancient Egypt and the subtle balance between the simple and the complex in classic Greek temples to sense the intellectual and spiritual character of the people who built them.

No better example of this exists than in the development of ancient Japanese architecture. One finds in Ise, Nara and Kyoto a profusion of structures and settings to prove how enduringly strong and "modern" has been the marriage between the given environment and the man-conceived additions to it.

The American sculptor Isamu Noguchi has the eyes to see that:

. . . the true roots of Japanese architecture lie in the Japanese relationship to nature. I venture to say that the understanding of wood is more important even than the resultant skill in its structural uses, however much it may please us to recognize the similarities between Japanese methods of wood construction and our own steel engineering. And stone is likewise stone.

He describes how easily, how naturally Japanese design established basic harmony with its surroundings:

What is the significance of those magnificent temple roofs that rise out of the landscape?... Their enclosure is like a sanctuary, a dominant object in negative space. The grand shrines of Ise are like boats on a beach. The fact of enclosure, not the bare space enclosed, is significant. In these sacred structures the function of the roof may be said to be hierarchic and linked to the land as a whole more than to its own immediate space.

In the plazas, squares, boulevards and promenades, in palaces and temples, is displayed the calligraphy of each people's culture, clearly spelling out what they most devoutly serve, sacred or profane.

History helps us to understand man by recording what he has committed himself to serve. A thousand years ago a highly sophisticated culture flourished in our Southwest, producing multistory masonry complexes of dwelling units and community facilities, which lasted for a score of centuries until apparently abandoned for unknown causes. Evidence, however, points to the abandonment as a result of soil exhaustion and the death of forests, with resulting fatal drought—conditions not much different from those prevalent today. Yet the finest structures of the Chacoan era show a highly developed and enlightened way of life, marked by a strong sense of the aesthetic.

The record of the new race of Americans who have worked on the land for the last three hundred years is a trail of desolation that we have left as we have chopped and burned and gouged our way across the country.

Just as every civilization has left its mark of greatness, we too have made great gains in disease control and physical comfort. Yet we have also succeeded in producing tools and commodities that are in themselves environment destroyers. Our contributions to the total environment so far have left only a negative record.

If we are not a great people, with a potential of magnificence to match the fury of our busyness, then we have a good deal of accounting to do for the enormous changes that the years of our dominance have witnessed. If we have the courage to know the stuff of which we are made—and the results of such knowledge are not yet clear—we must come to a recognition of what it is we serve.

My editor, as mentioned, insisted that behind any American aesthetic that may exist lies commerce, not art; that what we have built has been in the service of profit; and he implied that if we have been guided by a social vision it has been that of the right to be left alone. Coupled with our false sense of independence, monetary profit certainly has been our stimulus and guide. Our current impulse for planning has come largely through an appreciation of its value to the economy. The profit motive has been made so much a part of our sense of natural purpose — what's good for commerce and industry is good for America — that consumption of products is no longer based solely on economic necessity but has become a social duty.

I was born in Rush County, Indiana, where hand-split rails from solid black-walnut logs laid up in snake fences surrounded my uncle's farm, where maple syrup was taken from our trees in the lower forties, when the sap ran each spring, and boiled in open vats. Then, four out of five people lived on farms, and the tempo of our excitement could be caught in the hoofbeats of a trotting filly. Today, four out of every five people live in cities. Black-walnut logs are almost as difficult to obtain as the gold in the vaults at Fort Knox, and the Rush County farm is a subdivision. The tempo of our times is caught in the rapidly passing roar of the supersonic jet.

Worldly possessions, from cleansers and cars to homes and office buildings, are expendable. We have arranged things so that we think we must keep producing, consuming and producing again to survive. Our inventiveness has turned upon us to yield a population explosion, an automobile invasion, mass-education gigantism, television-age persuasion and a general environmental suffocation.

If there is something healthy in all this it is our deep-seated if secret dissatisfaction with what we have made for ourselves. Some of us scurry to the suburbs to escape the city while others flock to the city to escape the farms. To find security some of us conform while others, hating the monotony of mass-produced products and services, seek what seems to be different but is usually just another form of conformity. We are restless, nervous, compulsive, in search of something better. Something is missing; we aren't sure what. This is healthy, not as an ultimate way of life, but as a symptom of our longing for a better accommodation to our environment. Those very characteristics that mark us Americans — our plunging, brash exuberance, our unquenchable optimism in the face of doubt — are strengths that can shape an environmental art form. Since the aesthetic is a combination of function and special feeling, we can look

to our great freeways, airports and cities for our aesthetic. If our great structures are built in the service of monetary profit, so be it, so long as we find that the long-range capital gains lie in what is beautiful and that we can serve both profit and beauty. The Great Wall of China was built for military defense, in the service of war. It remains an awesome record of superhuman achievement.

Desire for monetary profit is only one of man's values, and we must work with the tools we have to achieve standards of which we can be proud. What impulses drive our people toward achievement? Brotherhood, spirituality, love and generosity might provide a spark but the profit motive is the driving force. Let's use it to its fullest. One does not realize a dream out of the stuff of dreams, but one can make a dream come true with the tools of reality.

One of our harshest realities is the current imbalance of our population. In less than a century we have seen the ratio of rural to city dwellers shift enormously, from 85 percent to 15 percent in favor of the rural dweller to the reverse proportion. And the 85 percent of our people who now live in our cities occupy only 15 percent of our available land space. This has created severe stresses in our society, especially in the task of making our rapidly expanding, overpopulated cities livable. Compounding the problem is the rapidity of this movement. Our enormous country is still largely undeveloped and is governed mainly by factors of mobility and communication. As local and regional areas have become closely interconnected in their needs and problems, we are forced to deal with population imbalance on a nationwide scale. Artificial boundaries such as city limits or state lines lose their meaning in the face of such pressures. Through transcontinental pipelines, waterways, power lines, highways, railways and air routes, our traditional territorial demarcations and governmental jurisdictions have been superseded by technology. Goods and services, from crude oil in pipelines to flowers delivered by wire, move with transcontinental speed and ease, to be clogged on arrival by local traffic jams. In five hours people can move from one coast to the other, or can spend the same five hours behind the wheel of a car, in a traffic snarl, breathing noxious gases, fruitlessly struggling with the distances of suburbia. Compulsive mobility has shattered boundaries. Whether local governments like it or not, our technological and social evolution is redefining political units strictly in terms of ecologically uniform regions. Cities and their suburbs spill over their own and state boundaries. In a rear-guard, after-the-fact effort, multistate agencies are formed to solve the symptoms of this new phenomenon—

such as polluted water and air flowing from state to state — instead of correcting them at their sources.

We can determine the shape and size of these regions only according to what we do with our environment. California, for example, is our fastest growing state. It is the most populous and the third largest in size. Alongside lies Nevada, a state two-thirds the size of California and containing a population only 2 percent of California's. Basically, the two states have the same problems of obtaining sufficient water and putting usable land to proper use. Ecologically, they belong together as a single, viable unit. If the line that separates them was artificial when it was first drawn, it is now much more so. To put it another way, our political boundary lines — marking off separate and often conflicting political jurisdictions — are not important when compared to the broader significance of the land on which they have been drawn.

And what of this land? Just as one can see its beauties from the air, one can also see its mutilation. Marks of natural erosion lie shaped in forms of sheer beauty, but other scars, carved by the press of an oversweeping population, remain as silent accusations against us.

This reflects a second harsh reality: a national point of view that has long needed changing. Our ecological history has been determined largely by the fact that immediately after establishing ourselves on the East Coast in the seventeenth century, we emerged into a national type unlike any other. Bent on mobility, and having the space for it, we have spent our short history in a series of major transitions. Underlying those changes has always been a sense of urgency. Our mobility was never peaceful, serene or dignified, but hasty and impelled by a sense of insecurity.

In trying to cope with the strains placed upon us by such rampant growth, we have generally adopted the "practical" point of view as being proper to a nation on the move. We have set aside our art, our great plazas and our buildings designed for beauty's sake as something belonging to "culture," something vaguely derivative and foreign, an expensive luxury to be bought with the excess of profits of commerce and industry.

Only recently, and still imperfectly, we have begun to sense the need for American commerce and industry to assimilate beauty, style, taste and good design in every phase of their operation in order to produce a gross national product that would include on a perpetual-yield basis the income from a major capital investment in an acceptable environment.

The Hopi Indians knew, for instance, that nature was infused with Deity; that every mountain stream or waterfall embodied a spirit. Contrast this with the scream of a chain saw ripping through stands of trees, killing whole forests so that lines of poles and cross-hatchings of wires can permit unhampered communication. "Man is a stream whose source is hidden," said Emerson. At that source lie vast reservoirs of progressive spirit, long untapped. However volatile our culture may be, the power to control our environment and the scientific miracles of our day is within our reach. There is no need to waste time feeling sorry for ourselves. Only in tempo, volume and contemporaneousness does our period in history vary from the past. Our peril lies not in the possession of enormous power, but in the abuse of it.

It is significant that Lewis Mumford, a serious student of our environment, is greatly concerned with our runaway, compulsive commitment to an uncontrolled tool-making, product-consuming economy. He outlines the transition in this way:

Our age is passing from the primeval state of Man marked by his invention of tools and weapons for the purpose of achieving mastery over forces of nature, to a radically different condition, in which he will not only have conquered but detached himself completely from the organic habitat. With this new macrotechnology, Man will create a uniform, all-enveloping structure, designed for automatic operation.

Instead of functioning actively as a tool-using animal, Man will become passive, a machine-serving animal whose proper functions, if this process continues unchanged, will either be fed into a machine, or strictly limited and controlled for the benefit of depersonalized collective organization.

As our population multiplies, our capacity to work is threatened, and with the loss of meaningful work we may lose our spiritual incentive.

Such are the liabilities we must convert into assets. Fortunately, there are other realities of a more positive nature. For one thing, becoming is still our way of life, which means, optimistically, that we have the power to become great.

The genius of our people has manifested itself in ways that indicate that our true nature, when we give it freedom to work, can be directed so that aesthetic values may be incorporated into our struggle for physical survival.

We have unique attributes of energy, ingenuity, optimism and generosity that can produce a new aesthetically based national ethic. These attributes can be directed toward influencing our environment and used in the service of husbanding our natural resources. In turn, this means that

we have the power to replace our preoccupation with tools and their products with a concern for the environment itself.

We can yet readjust our land-use concepts so as to place our land in trusteeship for the benefit of coming generations. Finally, to aid us we have the best lessons that the past can provide. From the present we can draw on our knowledge and skills, on our confidence that we still may choose and on our faith in our ability to work miracles. And the present offers us our greatest resource, a youthful generation for whom we must provide direction to the work at hand.

Placing the realities beside our goals, we can see that our dream is not unattainable, but that success is far from certain. There is little time left, and all too often an oversupply of confidence breeds delay. But if we seize our chance now we can yet salvage what we have damaged, save what is still unspoiled, and fashion an environment befitting the dignity of man.

That is what the American aesthetic is about. The search for ways to achieve it is the substance of this book.

Little Painted Desert, south of the Hopi Mesas, Arizona.

In seeking an aesthetic by which to live and build, we ought to be clear about what we want to avoid. Unfortunately, much of what we want to avoid we have already created, so our search in part means threading our way through the labyrinth of unaesthetic decisions made at crucial times in our development. Alfred North Whitehead reminds us that "the major advances in civilization are processes that all but wreck the societies in which they occur."

USE AND MISUSE OF POWER

Never before in history has a people possessed such abundant power to shape its environment. Using it piecemeal, without plan, we have done almost irreparable damage with this power. Our present inability to evaluate our efforts objectively, with no clear conviction as to what is good and what is bad, stems from a basic lack of confidence in ourselves, which in turn stems from a national feeling of cultural inferiority to Europe. We have always doubted ourselves. The belief that we don't measure up to the aesthetic standards of the Old World has haunted us and has contributed to our aesthetic imbalance. To compensate, we cover up by boasting. We fall back upon our so-called pride in material accomplishments as measured in our industrial growth, the rapid settlement of our land, our housing starts, our burgeoning cities, and our cleverness in reducing time and distance in mobility and communications.

What twinges of conscience we feel are stilled through a wide variety of forms of self-delusion, through advertising media, academic symposia, and seminars—great surges of words designed to tranquilize, not cure. This doesn't quite silence that persistent inner voice. We continue to cast critical inward glances and to admit privately that there is something we have neglected. We begin again to struggle against what we have made in America and our conscience begins anew to activate the search for an aesthetic dimension.

DERIVED FROM THE LANDSCAPE

Broad guidelines for community planning can be found in our landscape. Much of our immense country is lush and probably no other continent exceeds it in magnificent natural features. The elements of these features combine to demonstrate certain natural principles of spatial relationships and forms that are applicable to our efforts to create man-made oases. The juxtaposition of dense forests (those we have allowed to survive) with the great network of rivers reveals an intricate system of checks and balances relating to mass and mobility and to the inexorable workings of geophysics.

Our plains and mountains suggest ways in which growing population centers and large open spaces can be related. Anyone born in the American West and who has traversed the arid sweep of the Great Plains knows the romantic implications of the water hole as a symbol of life. To it all living beings are drawn and at each water hole, symbolic or real, myriad lines of animal tracks and man-made trails converge to form a living petroglyph, affirming the water hole as the key to the interrelationship of creature, land and sky.

Just as the Indians of these plains and mesas left petroglyphs describing what they saw as the relationships between man and the spirits of nature, modern man is engraving a petroglyph, though of another kind, across the land according to his needs and desires. Our cities have become blurred images reflecting the convergence of people and their means of support. For all their complexity, modern cities are basically the water holes of the industrial age where people seek sustenance in trade, festival and worship. They lie athwart desired lines of mobility — waterways, highways, railways, airlines, power lines and pipelines — which cross and gather over the land to sustain the fabric covering the American nerve system. We Americans shift restlessly, uncertainly, from city to city, place to place like a swarm of bees circling in search of a place to hive, gaining neither comfort nor confidence from our choices or from the huckster's attempt at reassuring words.

Indian petroglyph. Canyon de Chelly. New Mexico.

Mass construction housing.

Pueblo Bonito, Chaco Canyon, New Mexico.

A KEY IDEA

Once in a great while an essential concept vital to man's well-being surfaces and shines out. One such idea is embodied in the ruins of the ancient pueblos. On these sites the two-thousand-year history of a successful society thrived in what we would call a hostile environment. Here men served the gregarious side of their nature by gathering in high-density cores, having worked out a cooperate agreement with each other and nature — nature being represented by a pantheon of natural gods — for sustenance and social enrichment. They gained both security in their homes and harmony with the immense open space that surrounded them. This cluster concept has surfaced again in the extraordinary popular acceptance of Moshe Safdie's pueblo, known as Habitat, at Montreal's Expo '67 and suggests that the principle of the stratified city strikes a responsive chord in twentieth-century man.

Doorway, Pueblo Bonito. [Laura Gilpin]

INCONGRUITIES

Our history seems to have been a rhythm of volcanic eruptions; of shock waves of environmental ravages in the wake of periods of industrial exploitation, occurring in ever shorter sequences. Henry Adams commented wryly upon the effects of these eruptions, remarking that

Nothing so revolutionary had happened since the year 300 ... power leaped from every atom ... impossibilities no longer stood in the way.... [man] had seen four impossibilities made actual—the ocean steamer, the railway, the electric telegraph, and the Daguerrotype.... He had seen the coal-output of the United States grow from nothing to three hundred million tons or more.... The railways alone approached the carnage of war; automobiles and firearms ravaged society, until an earthquake became almost a nervous relaxation.... He could see that this new American —the child of incalculable coal-power, chemical power, electric power, and radiating energy as well as of new forces yet undetermined—must be a sort of God compared with any former creation of nature. At the rate of progress since 1800, every American who lived into the year 2000 would know how to control unlimited power.

But on one point only did Adams' prediction err: control of that power we do not have, and without that control, our knowledge is our enemy.

In the last fifty years the rate of change has exceeded that of the five thousand years of recorded history in the natural sciences.

PEOPLE—THEIR SPIRIT, THEIR ENVIRONMENT

Aerial photographs taken along the East and West Coasts, or along the southern tip of the Great Lakes, linked together into an aerial mosaic, show a continuous pattern of farms, villages, cities and industrial complexes, all enmeshed in a scheme of highways, railroads, bays, rivers and ports. It seems clear that most of us want to live on or near water, on easy routes of mobility and communication, that are accessible to high-density urban areas. At issue is the question of accepting this natural trend and of organizing already established concentrations of people into exciting, stimulating, happy places to live. As a corollary we must define the role of the resultant open space, which consists of some 85 to 90 percent of the country, to separate out and agree on its vital functions. Instead of treating the open space as the residue left after we build our cities, we must organize it for the prime services it must provide. We must preserve the geophysical characteristics so as to maintain a balanced ecology to supply the growing demands of the world for food and fiber, and we must establish the wilderness as a spiritual refuge for man and a physical refuge for wildlife.

Also at issue is the quality and style of our living space — its accessibility and convenience.

We are justly proud of the genius of a people who could build the complicated multistoried skyscrapers that form the famed skylines of San Francisco, New York and Chicago, and the planes that convert a trip across the continent or ocean into a few hours of incongruous luxury. But in terms of true quality and proportion in depth, doesn't our boasted genius somehow have the tragicomic air of the false front of a saloon in a Western gold-rush town? Our vaunted skyscraper is really an isolated, "unhitched" effulgence

Air and water pollution, Lake Michigan.

mostly unrelated to a larger plan; and the ground trip to and from the air terminals of any of our major cities is proof enough, in time consumed and sights seen, that however luxurious things may be in heaven, there is much to be desired on earth.

I doubt that we really accept such incongruities. Rather I think that we ignore them and try to concentrate on the things we know and love, that we are familiar with, such as the brand name products that we feel have made America. When pressed, we will freely admit that there is much wrong with us—inconsistencies, incongruities—but we put these aside because we really do not know how to deal with them. We are a pragmatic people and insist on solid solutions.

If we accept some of the ideas outlined here as being "at issue," we can find a sense of relief in the discovery that we are not unique in our predicament. We will find that they who came before us were faced with equal or greater problems of mobility and place. To them each volcanic eruption must have been as awesome as the detritus thrown off by the modern forces of change are to us. What they did and did not do makes for invaluable instructions upon which we can build.

John Hancock Center, Chicago, topped-out at one hundred stories. [© Ezra Stoller (ESTO)]

Canyon de Chelly, New Mexico.

When the first European immigrants came to America in the early 1600's they found a primeval continent that two hundred years later appeared to Alexis de Tocqueville as "grave, serious and solemn . . . a turbulent and foggy ocean washed its shore . . . and the foliage of its woods was dark and gloomy . . . a thousand rivulets, undirected in their course by human industry . . . the fall of the trees overthrown by age, the rushing torrent of the cataract, the lowing of the buffalo, and the howling of the wind were the only sounds that broke the silence of nature."

Since most of the newcomers were agrarian, they had to clear the land of trees for fields and settlements. The forest was only a barrier to be removed, the "endless" wilderness an obstacle to be conquered.

The Virginia colonists were closely attached to the land. Many household needs were met by what the plantation itself produced; family life centered around the plantation, with its cluster of buildings set in organic relation to the surrounding fields and woodlands. Not until the population increased and land settlements pushed inland, or upstream along the rivers, were commercial towns needed and established.

New England provided another pattern of land development. The town was the central feature. Although it differed from the Southern plantation, its orientation was also toward the land. As a group, the settlers chose the site and laid out the town plan with care. In the center of the village was a 2- to 3-acre lot, held in common by the residents as open space. Surrounding this village green were the church, the minister's house, the school and the market place. The town then divided the rest of the land among its residents.

Such an arrangement not only demanded orderly development, but also created an automatic population control by setting a limit on the number of settlers that could take up residence in any particular town. Once the limit was reached, the orderly process would begin again in a new location. In this manner, New England set up a pattern of forced mobility.

Since road construction started slowly, trade depended for a long time on access to water. The first preliminary roadway between Boston and Plymouth was laid out in 1639. Colonial mail service between the major communities did not come for over thirty years. The few sections of the road that did exist were little more than paths wide enough for horseback travel, and even by 1750 the colonists were relying almost exclusively upon river transportation.

Rapid development and growth within the colonies during the first half of the eighteenth century made it clear, however, that improved roads were badly needed, and by the end of the century this sense of urgency had been translated into nearly 3,000 miles of road construction. But this was an achievement of quantity, not quality. The roads were "hazardous" and "wretched" because "such trees alone were cut down as were necessary for the formation of a road, or rather the line of a road, for this roadway was still in a very rude state, the driver being obliged to wind as well as he could between the remaining stumps. The soft soil being rendered deep by the rain that had fallen, our progress was very slow, not exceeding 13 miles in four hours."

In the late 1780's, experiments were made in the construction of short stretches of toll roads. Under charters from the colonies, private capital was attracted to these road projects and New England soon had a number of tollways, including much of the three post roads from New York to Boston. In 1792 the Philadelphia-Lancaster (72 miles away) turnpike was begun, the first long-distance American road surface with broken stone and gravel, and the first major land route into new lands west of the Eastern seaboard. With the success of this road a boom of turnpike construction began. In 1812, a through turnpike was completed between Philadelphia, then the largest city in America, and New York. By 1832, over 2,000 miles of road had been built, costing from $900 to $7,000 per mile.

Road building, even during that preliminary period, was pursued with little regard for values other than those of immediate success and profit. "The turnpike companies had an arrogant way of cutting straight for an objective, tearing up even cemeteries. They were given the eminent domain, so they got what they wanted. . . . In the cities they were regarded with respect, and there was a great deal of money in them, rather like a public utility; but in the country they were hated and feared."

Such increasing mobility of the early Americans, and the influx of immigrants during the 1700's, led to land speculation. English and American merchants and planters, as well as influential legislators, leaped at the opportunity to make substantial profits by purchasing vast tracts of the frontier wilderness for resale at greatly increased prices.

By the mid-1700's, as the tide of settlement began to move down the western slope of the Appalachian Mountains, and speculation substantially influenced the pattern of westward expansion. One of the largest land investment enterprises occurred in 1749, when nearly 2 million acres of virgin land were apportioned to prominent Virginia planter-politicians comprising six land-holding companies.

In the development of this first mobility explosion, three factors formed a pattern that would be repeated again and

New England village on Connecticut River.

again in our history. First, an innovation—in this case a road system—was made in an atmosphere of urgency to supply a huge and seemingly instant demand. Consequently, it was deemed more important to build as many miles of road as possible, just to get there, than to take extra time to maintain high quality.

Secondly, the roads were thrust forward in as straight a line as possible to lessen the distances traveled. There was little respect for what was already on the right of way, and the land itself was regarded only as something to be traversed.

Lastly, and most far-reaching in importance, it was accepted that national development would be a legitimate area for private speculation. Thus the question of tampering with an environment, an action in which a segment of the public would share for better or worse, became a matter of individual conscience. People who cared about the land and its ecology could only hope that speculators and builders would weigh their responsibility to future generations against their desires for immediate profit.

Shortly after our independence was won, the principle of a national "public domain" was established. In an action of rare unity, the states voluntarily ceded the vast forested lands beyond the Appalachians, much of which had been claimed by the individual colonies, to the national government, establishing a "national domain." This was probably the most important single act concerning land tenure in our history. In an attempt not only to stimulate settlement of the new region, but also to counteract the land speculators whose consciences were not reliable, a land ordinance was passed by Congress in 1785. This law—the first important federal legislation regarding the disposal of the public domain—provided for the survey and sale of the lands under a system of townships measuring 6 miles square and subdivided into 640-acre sections. This was the first instance of a large-scale survey actually preceding settlement, although the plan was reminiscent of the advance land planning by New England towns.

Meanwhile, the settlers became conditioned by the "endless" wilderness. They came to believe that beyond the horizon to the west there would always be another forest to cut for lumber, another valley to clear and farm, an endless abundance of resources, should the present forest become depleted through logging or fire, or should the soil erode or its nutrients be exhausted. This new attitude, spurred by improvements in the means of communication, resulted in wasteful practices and was contrary to basic principles of husbanding resources. Such prodigality was surprising considering that these principles were well observed in Europe, even by our pioneers before they came to America.

Settlement pushed inland, and short canals were built to supplement navigable parts of rivers, bypassing falls or rapids, to permit further westward penetration. As was the practice on privately built roads, tolls were collected from the users of the canals. An even greater opportunity was offered by connecting the Eastern river systems, such as the tributaries of the Monongahela and the Cheat Rivers, with those draining into the Mississippi, principally the Ohio. Samuel Morse observed that "when we have arrived at either of these western waters, the navigation through that immense region is opened in a thousand directions." Thus, at the end of the 1700's, though still struggling with the problems of finances and responsibility for such internal improvements, America was poised for a breakthrough to the Western lands.

In 1784, General George Washington, writing to Virginia Governor Benjamin Harrison, had spoken of another reason for binding the country together with routes of communications: "I need not remark to you, Sir, that the flanks and rear of the United States are possessed by other powers, and formidable ones, too; nor how necessary it is to apply the cement of interest to bind all parts of the Union together by indissoluble bonds, especially that part which lies immediately west of us. The Western States (I speak now from my own observation) hang upon a pivot. The touch of a feather will turn them any way."

The strongest powers in Europe claimed and held the heart of the continent, and the new United States would need that heart to become a first-class power.

Two events then occurred which influenced drastically the direction of the new country. In 1787 a small steam-driven craft was successfully propelled against the current of the Delaware River. While most people thought the inventor, John Fitch, a fool, John Stevens, an American lawyer and inventor, could see in those first puffs of steam a new force for the growth of America: "You see what a steam engine can do for a boat. The time is coming, and soon, when it will do greater things on land. This new nation will be developed by the power of steam." Before long, steam mobility transformed the Mississippi River into a major transportation route. In 1815 when a steamboat went upriver from New Orleans to Louisville in twenty-five days, a new era in American trade and internal development began, for now the most important link in the developing Midwest lay to the south. As a result, from 1830 to 1840 New Orleans was the fastest-growing city on the continent.

Appalachian Mountains, Pennsylvania.

Water transportation made mobility our greatest force for national growth. The waterfronts of the commercial trade centers were lined with wharves and warehouses. At St. Louis alone the number of steamboats serving the trade center rose from 80 in 1832 to over 5,000 in 1860. In 1852, some 500 westward-bound migrants were packed onto a single vessel headed up the Mississippi from New Orleans. The peak year of 1855 saw 3 million people travel on the Ohio River.

The second event was the purchase from France, in April, 1803, of the Louisiana Territory. Of incalculable value to us, this acquisition doubled the area of the nation and would in time yield the states of Louisiana, Arkansas, Missouri, Iowa, Minnesota, Oklahoma, Kansas, Nebraska, North and South Dakota, Colorado, Wyoming and Montana, at a price of $15 million.

President Jefferson, in 1804, commissioned two Army officers, Meriwether Lewis and William Clark, to lead an overland expedition up the Missouri River, over the Rocky Mountains, to the Pacific Northwest to find a water route from the Missouri to the Pacific. This federally financed project was completed a year and a half later when the party reached the mouth of the Columbia River. Jefferson's chief motivation for promoting federal assistance to improve internal transportation at that time was the development of this prize of new territory. In 1808 Jefferson's wise Secretary of the Treasury, Albert Gallatin, prepared an extensive report for Congress, urging federal financing of a nationwide system of canals, river improvements and turnpikes, at a cost of $20 million, to be financed over a ten-year period. Funds for this program were to come from the surplus then existing in the federal treasury and from the sale of public domain lands. Congress balked, and the only tangible result of the proposal was the National Road, which ran from Cumberland, Maryland, to Vandalia, Illinois, and which was constructed with federal money at an initial cost of $7 million. This single road, extending across the heart of the Midwest, stretched 834 miles. A mule-powered Fresno Scraper, probably the forerunner of the bulldozer, was used to build the road, which soon became crowded with traffic: horsedrawn coaches, great freight wagons, horses, mules, cattle, sheep and pigs, traffic which was, according to a contemporary source, "visible all day long at any point." New towns, which often began as inns and toll stops, were soon springing up along the road.

Even then the issue of federal participation in such projects was open to contention. John Quincy Adams, seeing far into the past and future, favored internal improvements made with federal help:

To the topics of internal improvements...I recur with peculiar satisfaction. It is that from which I am convinced that the unborn millions of our posterity who are in future ages to people this continent will derive their most fervent gratitude to the founders of the Union.... The magnificence and splendor of their public works are among the imperishable glories of the ancient republics. The roads and aqueducts of Rome have been the admiration of all after ages, and have survived thousands of years. Some diversity of opinion has prevailed with regard to the powers of Congress for legislation upon objects of this nature. But nearly 20 years have passed since the construction of the first national road was commenced. The authority for its construction was then unquestioned. To how many thousands of our countrymen has it proved a benefit!

But President Andrew Jackson brought federal financing to a halt when he vetoed federal aid to Kentucky's Marysville Turnpike in 1830. This forced the turnpike companies to rely upon private financing, as private corporations rather than as public utilities, though Kentucky ultimately paid half the $426,000 cost of this project.

With the steamboat rapidly strengthening the bond between the South and the developing Midwest territories, Eastern business interests pushed for east-west water routes even though turnpikes and toll and post roads had already begun to tie together many parts of the interior.

To compete with Maryland's roads, Baltimore's fast-sailing Baltimore Clipper, and Pennsylvania's Turnpike, New York State authorized and financed construction of the Erie Canal, which was completed in 1825. Although this water route was frozen out of operation during the winter months, the favorable economy of the canal's mass carrying capacity still won out and post road towns lost ground to canal towns. The new form of mobility brought new prosperity. Goods transported by the old Buffalo-to-New York post road cost $100 per ton, delivered in twenty days; by the canal, $15 per ton in just eight days. The success of the Erie Canal caused a canal boom in the 1820's and the 1830's.

In spite of the economic advantages, the costs of canal construction were too great for the states, especially for the frontier states. Private investors in the East and in England therefore subscribed to state bond issues, and Congress encouraged the canal boom by giving the states alternate sections of land from the public domain, 5 miles wide on each side of the canal right-of-way. Speculators, from the East Coast to the Mississippi Valley, moved in at once to take advantage of such a windfall. The federal "handout" of land grants to the canal companies formed an important precedent and generated bitter arguments; however, it was clear that in the case of the canals, the incentive system worked to the benefit of all concerned.

At this time, but in what might as well have been a different world, another crucial event was taking place. In 1826, twenty-eight-year-old Jedediah S. Smith was leading a group of fur traders southwestward from Bear River Valley in northern Utah. They crossed the forbidding Mojave Desert, penetrated the San Bernardino Mountains and found a hospice in the Mission of San Gabriel, which had been established by the Spanish Franciscan friars on the Pacific Coast in the seventeenth century. Smith and his men were the first known white men to cross these barriers overland into California and were the forerunners of a great migration following the discovery of gold in California twenty-two years later.

As primitive trails were being extended into the vast wilderness of the West, iron rails were being laid in the East. In 1830 the initial 14 miles of the Baltimore & Ohio were opened. At first, horsepower was used. Then the B.&O. directors tried sails, but the wind proved unreliable. Again steam won the day. In 1836, near Philadelphia, an American-built wood-burning steam locomotive demonstrated its ability to negotiate a steep grade while pulling a load of freight.

The Baltimore & Ohio had been formed to compete with the canals, and it was to be expected that this company and other railroads would be opposed by the canal interests. However, substantial opposition arose out of an even more fundamental concern: the shattering effect of the steam engine on the environment. Many people were angered by the noise and the dirt, as well as by the apparent disruption of pastoral America.

To the historian Henry Adams the old universe was being discarded, the pastoral idea of America was being threatened by this machine that multiplied by many times the forces man had previously had in his grasp. What was happening was the beginning of the transformation of life by machine technology. Adams perceived that with the advent of the steam engine there had arisen a violent conflict between the machine and the natural environment, in which the American aesthetic was being threatened by mechanical utility.

Many other writers of the period reflected this shock. Henry David Thoreau resentfully described the shrill whistle of a train invading the natural world of Walden Pond;

PUBLIC POST ROADS 1774

MAIN POST ROADS 1834

and Nathaniel Hawthorne, in the woods near Concord, Massachusetts, also reacted to the unmistakable sound:

But hark! there is the whistle of the locomotive—the long shriek—harsh, above all other harshness, for the space of a mile cannot mollify it into harmony. It tells a story of busy men, citizens, from the hot street, who have come to spend a day in a country village, men of business; in short of all unquietness; and no wonder that it gives such a startling shriek, since it brings the noisy world into the midst of our slumbrous peace.

The railroad was also converting some of the best lands to freight yards and railroad lines. Artist Thomas Cole bemoaned the loss of beauty along the Hudson River to the ambitions of "dollar-godding utilitarians" who "are cutting down all the trees in the beautiful valley."

Waterfront lands, parks and cemeteries, as well as historic buildings and homes, were destroyed by the railroad, as others had been by the first wave of turnpike and toll-road construction, and as still others would be in the mid-twentieth-century expressway boom.

The steam locomotive—associated with fire, smoke, speed, iron and noise—was, however, the leading symbol of America's rapidly increasing industrial power. To many, the railroad was the emblem not only of American progress but of the advancement of the human race. To extend iron (and, later, steel) rails farther across the landscape became a national obsession. Thomas Carlyle, on a visit to the United States, saw the need for a balance between the machinery of mobility and the urban and rural environments. To him, the railroad was a centrifugal force that threatened to break down, once and for all, the conventional contrast between these two styles of life. Time and space were being drastically reduced; and traditional boundaries between the city and the countryside were being ruptured.

As rail construction took the nation by storm, and the railroads satisfied more and more of the nation's passenger- and freight-carrying needs, the public roads in the East were neglected for half a century and fell into disrepair.

While railroads were helping to knit together the eastern half of the United States, the Santa Fe Trail, with its eastern terminus at Independence, Missouri, was being carved into the land. By 1860, some three thousand wagons and nine thousand men were employed in the trail's trade. In 1841, the first settlers' caravan left St. Louis, heading for the West Coast via a more northerly route up the Platte River Valley in Nebraska, later to be known as the Oregon Trail. Two years later, more than a thousand Americans migrated to the Oregon Territory; 121 wagons, 698 oxen, 296 horses, 973 cattle, 260 men, 130 women and 620 children. In 1844 the Stevens-Murphy party succeeded in bringing wagons the entire distance from Missouri to California, west of the Sierra Nevada.

Discovery of gold in 1848 triggered a mass migration to California. Historian Robert Glass Cleland has written: "The immense volume of travel over the main emigrant routes turned the faintly defined trails of the fur traders into dusty, deeply rutted thoroughfares, visible for miles on the prairies or across the white alkaline face of the desert."

Migration to the West Coast was further stimulated when California became a United States territory in 1848 and the thirty-first state in 1850. California's northern cities grew swiftly because of the gold rush. San Francisco "seemed to have accomplished in a day the growth of half a century," observed one resident in 1850. California's first railroad, built in 1854, was laid in the redwood country. Within a few years, rail lines penetrated the forests, hauling out the ancient trees in gigantic sections—one per railroad flatcar.

Mid-nineteenth-century transportation in the West was by saddle horse, pack train, and heavy wooden-wheeled ox-carts. Goods brought to California by steamboat around the Horn or transferred at Panama were redistributed by wagon trains to western settlements as far as Utah, Idaho and Wyoming. At the peak of this era of mobility in the West, at least five thousand multi-make or freight wagons were in use.

By 1850 over 9,000 miles of railroad track crisscrossed the Eastern states. Now lines were being extended westward toward the prairies and plains. During the following decade tracklaying accelerated to an average of 2,000 miles a year, an increase of 560 percent over the 1840's.

This growth was spurred by the federal government through grants in aid of construction. The first such grant was made in 1851, when the Illinois Central Railroad was given authority "in perpetuity" to build and operate a 700-mile line from Cairo to Dunleith (now East Dubuque, Iowa) with a "spur" line to Chicago.

By the second half of the 1800's celebrants of the machine were beginning to take the offensive. Americans were transforming a vast wilderness into an industrial and commercial civilization, with the machine in the central role as the motivating force. Daniel Webster said of the railroad that it "towers above all other inventions of this or the preceding age." He admitted that the steam engine disturbed the peace of the rural environment and that "it injures the look of fields. But I have observed . . . that the railroad directors and railroad projectors are no enthusiastic lovers of landscape beauty. Their business is to cut and slash, to level and deface a finely rounded field, and fill up beautifully winding valleys. They are quite utilitarian in their creed and in their practice. Their business is to make good roads." Webster was among those who valued the qualities of rural life but, captivated by the rapid changes in an age he called miraculous, he also agreed with the advocates of serious machine enterprises that these inventions would increase the material wealth of the country.

The introduction of the power loom in 1814 affected American industry profoundly, especially in the manufacture of textiles, through the introduction of a mechanical power to replace human power. This was the first stage of the continuing process of automation. A textile mill at Waltham, Massachusetts, installed the new machine, which brought all factory operations under one roof. The manufacture of iron was also transformed by technology in the early 1800's. With the westward expansion of industry and population, Pittsburgh — strategically situated on routes of mobility — became the "Iron City of America," a center of rolling mills, foundries and (later) great smoking blast furnaces. The near-exhaustion of the Eastern forests by the 1840's encouraged the use of coal for firing the furnaces, and men such as Andrew Carnegie ruthlessly proceeded to build great industrial empires, bringing together under their control vast iron-ore and coal deposits, Great Lakes barges and entire railroad systems.

In 1832 Samuel F. B. Morse, aided by Ezra Cornell, discovered a way to send messages electromagnetically, thereby creating instantaneous communication. The first message —"What hath God wrought" (sent in coded dot and dash impulses)—was successfully transmitted over the wire in 1844. Proclaimed the New York *Herald*: "The telegraph is unquestionably the greatest invention of the age."

The revolutionary effect of this increased technology on human values was sensed by de Tocqueville as early as 1840: "To minds thus predisposed, every new method which leads by a shorter road to wealth, every machine which spares labor, every instrument which diminishes the cost of production, seems to be the grandest effort of the human intellect."

President Millard Fillmore expressed the prevailing optimism: "We live in an age of progress. Our territory is checkered over with railroads, and furrowed with canals. And the numerous applications for patents for valuable improvements distinguish this age and its people from all others. The whole country is full of enterprise." Love of progress, as long as it was material progress, became part of the American spirit. Some Americans, however, called the growing industrialization and mobility calamitous. They could see that the Industrial Revolution was producing more in America than exciting inventions. The factory system was accompanied by abuse of human resources in the forms of poor working conditions, low wages and employment of children. Immigrants, imported to do the equivalent of slave labor, poured into the country at the rate of over 5 million during the 1880's. New York and Chicago both became highly urbanized industrial centers with populations of a million and over in the decade between 1880 and 1890.

The Industrial Revolution automatically produced blight, pollution, disease, despair and slums.

Indiana's Booth Tarkington described the death of a town in a popular novel of the 1920's:

. . . for the town was growing and changing as it had never grown and changed before. It was heaving up in the middle incredibly; and as it heaved and spread, it befouled itself and darkened its sky. Its boundary was mere shapelessness on the run . . . a farm had become a suburb which would immediately shoot out other suburbs into the country . . . as the town grew, it grew dirty, with an incredible completeness . . . it was the fault of the idealist, who said, "The more dirt, the more prosperity."

Edward Hungerford wrote of traveling by train into Chicago from the East: "To the right and to the left long vistas with ungainly outlines of steel mills with unturned rows of smoking stacks, of gas holders and of packing houses."

As the railroads fought to secure their share of the hard-coal business, they pushed their rails farther and farther into the rich anthracite fields, and along their tracks dreary industrial settlements arose. The industrial giants were having their own way, unhampered by income taxes or conscience. Company towns were established near St. Louis, Chicago, Pittsburgh and New York. Grim rows of rigidly packed employee barracks surrounded giant mills. The grime and pall of the mill towns symbolized the age, in sharp contrast to the cleanliness of the water-powered mill towns of earlier years. Novelist Rebecca Harding Davis described the industrial Wheeling, West Virginia, of the mid-1800's:

The idiosyncrasy of this town is smoke. It rolls sullenly in slow folds from the great chimneys of the iron foundries and settles down in black, slimy pools on the muddy streets. Smoke of the wharves, smoke in the dingy boats, on the yellow river — clinging in a coating of greasy soot to the housefront, to faded poplars, the faces of the passersby.

Gold dredge tailings, Snelling, California.

By the 1880's, the flight to the suburbs began, for those who could afford it, and such satellites as Greenwich, Connecticut, Chestnut Hill, Pennsylvania, and Lake Forest, Illinois, were formed by the wealthy as a refuge against the industrial blight that was creating their riches. From the Atlantic seaboard to the Mississippi River American industrial drive had thrown a network of iron rails across the land, tying city to city, farmland to city, mine to mill and virgin forest to sawmill—30,000 miles of it in all, built in thirty years.

But something quite different had happened at the one-hundredth meridian, when the heretofore successful pioneers confronted the semi-arid Great Plains.

How and why this happened goes to the heart of the shaping of the American aesthetic. Geography intimately influences a people's ideas about land and space and determines what will be done with them. This is especially relevant to the American aesthetic, because we are one of the few nations of the modern world dedicated to mobility. For the most part, the basic patterns of our Eastern lands were established by the newly arrived; that is, by those who had literally just got off the boat or the wagon, or those who were first- or second-generation native residents. This is in sharp contrast with the European peoples who tended to stay rooted to their communities, at least until the Industrial Revolution.

Fort Union on the Santa Fe Trail. Note wagon trails still visible today.

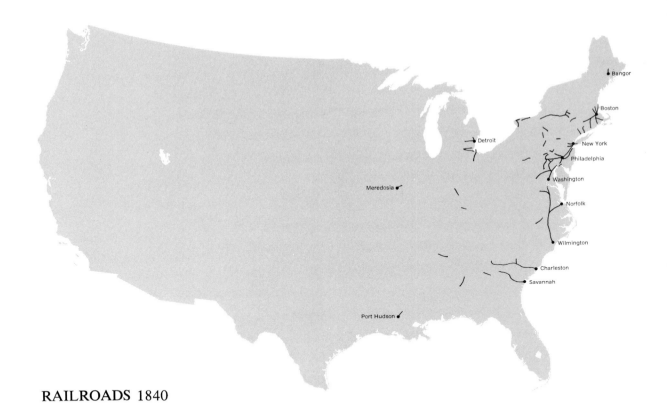

RAILROADS 1840

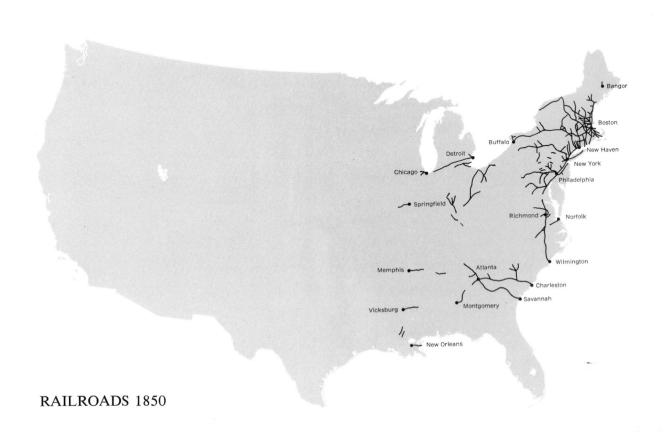

RAILROADS 1850

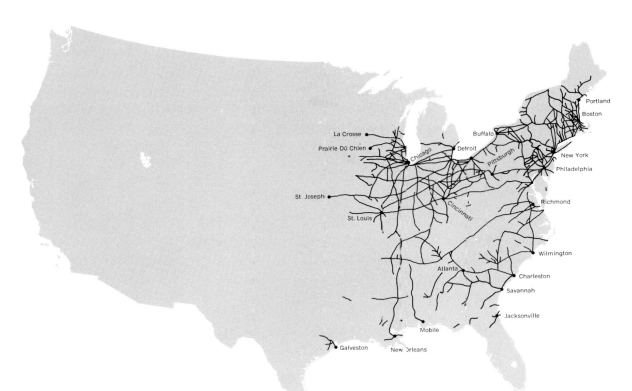

RAILROADS 1860

RAILROADS 1870

51

The settlers who first populated our land east of the Mississippi were Europeans whose roots were in lands not unlike the Eastern United States. America's profusion of rivers, dense forests, steep or gentle hills, truncated beaches and good harbors, and weather that had a tendency toward high humidity with regular snows and rainfalls, made up an environment such as they had also known in France, Germany, Britain, Scandinavia—most of Europe. Above all, they were used to limited vistas—there was always a stand of trees or a hill or a mountain to contour the horizon. In Europe this kind of geography influenced the establishment of relatively small territorial domains, whether farms, estates or cities. Travel could be long by our standards, but not prohibitively so, and variations between mountains and valleys, rivers and forests, flatlands and hills lent relief to the eye and stimulation to the spirit. The Europeans had learned to handle such a geography reasonably. Though the Eastern American landscape was similar, the forests were dense and more dangerous, and the Southern climate more oppressively hot. But, in the main, the geography was the same.

Then, when they crossed the Mississippi, they were confronted by the Great Plains; and beyond that, the great American desert. Here were enormous expanses of space, vistas stretching to the rim of the horizon, seas of grass, sagebrush and sand, broken only by precipitously rising mesas or plunging canyons. The grass was so tall a man got lost in it. The wind was an ever-present force sweeping down from the north, and there were storms that could kill with bludgeoning force. It was as if Western man had pushed westward—only to come upon the Russian steppes or the wastes of Mongolia.

The Spanish explorers of the seventeenth century had seen these expanses, of course, but they were looking for gold and they passed over the land as transients. But the Americans were settlers and not all of them could go the whole way to California and Oregon. Having made the commitment to go west, they would have to live off this alien land, and this time, space itself seemed an enemy to be conquered.

For these settlers, in their small numbers, the sense of isolation and loneliness was nearly overwhelming. In the East their parceling of the land had been influenced by natural land forms, by the courses of rivers or streams, by the rises of hills, by forbidding stands of forest. Except in the South, where plantation farming forced the clearing of great areas of land, territorial boundaries remained modest and reflected natural terrain.

South Carolina farm patterns.

Mount Katahdin, Maine.

Farms and section lines in the Plains States.

On the plains the need to impose order on the land seemed much greater. There was one main consideration — distance. On the plain roads could run straight, and they did, for the most part, stretching westward along the already well-worn tracks of the prairie schooners heading for California and Oregon. The straight line became the dominant motif. Parcels of land tended to be rectangular; the territories, which in time would become states, were often set as virtual rectangles. Barbed-wire fences repeated the motif. In their determination to subdue and win the West, Americans stretched forth their lines of mobility, stretched out other lines of aggrandizement to claim and parcel the land, stretched still other lines to protect and then to govern it, and of course enormous amounts of territory remained in the public domain.

What began as a reaction to a dramatic new challenge became a habit of mind. The West began to develop an aesthetic peculiar to its own.

In Walter Prescott Webb's words:

The spread of the range and ranch cattle industry over the Great Plains in the space of 15 years — the movement was fairly complete in ten or twelve — is perhaps one of the outstanding phenomena in American history. During that period and for ten years after, men, cattle and horses held almost undisputed possession of the region.

Meanwhile, many Californians were pressing for a rail link across the plains, deserts and mountains to connect with the Eastern rail system. In 1862, President Abraham Lincoln signed the Pacific Railroad Act, which subsidized construction of a transcontinental rail line to meet the Central Pacific Railroad being built eastward from San Francisco.

Railroads were generally financed by large amounts of private capital, by subsidies from state, county and local governments, and by large grants of land and loans from the national government.

In 1865, the Union Pacific Railroad was organized, and two years later construction began at Omaha, Nebraska. Originally it was expected that the Union Pacific line would meet the Central Pacific at the California border, but Central Pacific's directors were intent upon pushing their line as far east as possible, to increase its share of government grants and subsidies, including twenty sections, or over 12,000 acres of land, per mile of track. Competition between the two railroads spurred them on at ever-faster rates of construction. Both railroad companies obtained federal loans for railroad construction and land grants totaling 25 million acres and were given the right to issue stock up to $100 million.

On May 10, 1869, a ceremony was held at Promontory, Utah, to mark the spanning of the continent by the railroad.

In 1862, Congress passed and President Lincoln signed the Homestead Act, which was meant to encourage settlement of Western lands. Under this law, 160 acres of the public domain were offered free to each homesteader. After five years of residence or cultivation of the land, the homesteader could receive title, or he could purchase the land after only six months by paying $1.25 per acre. This sum applied impartially to all public-domain lands, whether they consisted of Nevada alkali flats, Great Plains grasslands or primeval forests. Most of the lands west of the hundredth meridian, however, were unlike the wetter regions of the Eastern part of the United States. Where 160 acres provided an adequate farm in the East, this acreage in the West was both too large for irrigated farming and too small for dry farming or raising of livestock.

With the opening of this vast region, speculation flourished as land monopolies rushed to take advantage of the opportunities. Land sales were often recorded fraudulently, as occurred in the great forests of coast redwoods in northern California. A practice was made of employing individuals to file claims that were then turned over to timber companies. Claims were often filed under fictitious names.

Always in the forefront of expansion that marked the latter half of the nineteenth century were the railroads, which were also certain to be at the source of the huge profits to be had. While 100 million acres of public lands were disposed of under the Homestead Act, even more than that—some 125 million—went to the railroads as allotments along their right of way. (These grants of alternate sections of land also enhanced the value of the lands retained by the government; the price was doubled, from $1.25 per acre to $2.50.) In addition, for each mile of track Congress granted substantial loans of money toward construction. Thus, for example, the Northern Pacific Railroad benefited enormously by the huge grants of land from the public domain. This railroad alone received close to 40 million acres—an area larger than Pennsylvania and New Jersey combined. Much of the land was subsequently traded for rich timberlands in the Pacific Northwest, under a provision in the 1897 "Scripper Act."

Thus the railroads became a central power not only in the processes of mobility but in the campaign of exploitation of natural resources that quickly ensued.

FEDERAL LAND GRANTS FOR THE CONSTRUCTION OF RAILROADS AND WAGON ROADS

1823-1871

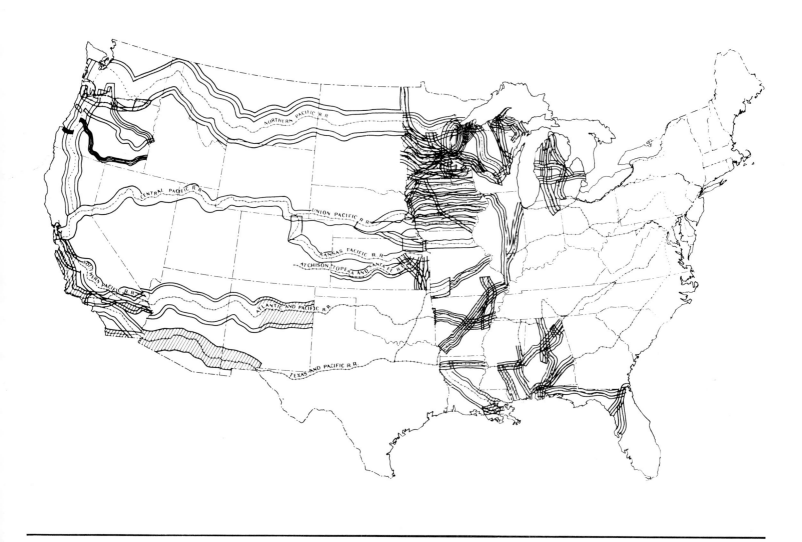

Areas within "primary" and "indemnity" limits of *unforfeited* Federal land grants for railroads and wagon roads. The maximum amount of land obtainable was one-half that within the primary limits, the lands granted being in the alternate survey sections. The maximum was often not obtained.

Areas within "primary" and "indemnity" limits of *unforfeited* Federal land grants for railroads and wagon roads. The maximum amount of land obtainable was one-half that within the primary limits.

Grant limits.

Courtesy of the Bancroft Library,
University of California, Berkeley

By the mid-nineteenth century, strands of mobility lines and the gatherings where they crossed began to pattern the vastness of the American landscape. Because the railroad preceded almost all settlement in the West, new towns sprang up along the rail routes. Those located in closest harmony with the needs of the settlers were destined to burgeon into perceptible core cities. In 1854, for example, C. K. Holliday moved to the territory of Kansas with two ambitions: to establish a town and to build a railroad. The town, Topeka, grew so rapidly that it soon became the territorial capital. The railroad he envisioned crossed the great scenic Southwest, along the old Santa Fe Trail. It was chartered as the Atchison, Topeka & Santa Fe Railroad in 1859, by the Kansas territorial legislature, and construction began at Kansas City. By 1881, the Santa Fe met the Southern Pacific thrusting from California to form the second transcontinental rail link. In 1883, the Santa Fe succeeded in completing its own line to California; this route from Chicago to the Pacific is still the only railroad spanning the entire distance on its own right of way.

In 1870, the crucial marriage between mobility and technology was consummated when, for the first time, a train was run successfully coast to coast, from Boston to San Francisco. The trip took eight days, but by 1880 the time had been trimmed to a mere three and a half days, a record not to be outdone for thirty years, when the time dropped slightly to half an hour under three days. In this age of five-hour transcontinental crossings, we may lose sight of the significance of those records. But when we recall that only ten years before that eight-day journey of 1870 the pioneers had had to spend as much as four months along the trails to Oregon and California, we can see that the railroad made possible an improvement in mobility far more significant than the telescoping of time made possible by the jet.

By the turn of the century, a major transformation had occurred across the face of the land. In a brief several decades, a few hundred miles of unconnected stretches of railroad had expanded to an efficient network knitting the regions of the continent together and totaling nearly 250,000 miles of track. The nation's lines of mobility were filling in, setting the pattern of our life as a people.

Under the influence of new means of travel, a flood of settlement ensued. In one decade—the 1860's—Missouri's population increased by nearly 50 percent, Iowa's by nearly 80 percent, Minnesota's by over 150 percent, the Dakota Territory's by over 200 percent, Kansas's by 240 percent and Nebraska's by more than 325 percent. Grime, pollution, population saturation and faulty urbanization were forcing increasing numbers of city dwellers to travel to the West, either to start anew in better surroundings or simply to enjoy the clean air and open spaces for a while. What attracted them was something very much a part of the American dream: the freedom expressed in broad vistas, the compelling beauty of nature's color and forms.

Through accounts written at the time, we can still glimpse what they saw. In September, 1883, the Northern Pacific brought an explorer to the Dakota Territory who, it was said later, "did more to change land-use practices in the West than anyone else in American history." Theodore Roosevelt, in the words of one biographer, arrived in the Bad Lands in the last days of its wilderness, while it was still a "land of vast silent places, of lonely rivers, and of plains where the wild game stared at the passing horseman." It was that time of transition when old-timers who revisited the area could notice two important changes. "The Indian villages, with their tepees and copper-colored inhabitants, had given way to the white man's towns, and the buffalo, once darkening the prairie from the Red River to the Rio Grande, had dwindled from a multitude of 50 million or more to a few scattered herds. In most other respects, the Bad Lands looked as they had since the exuberant days of the Pleistocene."

Other visitors were brought to the nation's Western parks and recreation areas by means of a line initiated in 1882 by the Northern Pacific to run to Yellowstone, which ten years before had been established as the country's first national park. Unfortunately, too many of the visitors were hunters, professional and self-styled, whose callous slaughter of the bison—often from moving trains—disastrously reduced the herds.

Those who came to settle brought about their own revolution. Railroad companies frequently promoted settlement by providing transportation and, as we have seen, laying out towns along the right of way. Among the immigrants brought West were farmers, whose products, they were assured, would be carried to market by the railroads.

Inevitably, conflict developed between the new farmers and the established cattle industry. The farmers demanded that the cattlemen fence their range lands, while the cattlemen bitterly fought the threat to their free, open range. Fencing the Great Plains presented a difficulty: there were virtually no natural materials with which to construct fences. Not until 1873 was a solution found, when the Industrial Revolution produced the barbed-wire fence, enabling the farmer to mark off and protect his lands cheaply, and helping to bring about the decline of the Great Plains cattle kingdom.

In the western, more arid part of the Great Plains, surface water was insufficient for farming needs, so that irrigation of crops in this region required tapping the water resources beneath the ground surface, drawing it through the use of windmills.

However, these problems were only part of a large condition of fundamental importance to our thinking as a people and to the development of our natural aesthetic. The hundredth meridian marked a crucial line separation for us. East of it was a climate of reliable precipitation and a landscape containing an extensive waterway system, again not dissimilar from the condition of Europe, where lay our traditions of culture, including agriculture. West of it lay a billion acres of comparatively level land marked both by a general lack of trees and insufficient rainfall for ordinary intensive agriculture.

These differences, especially the lack of rainfall, made of the hundredth meridian a "cultural fault." Practically every social and political established practice carried across this line was remade or greatly altered. Modes of travel, ways of tilling the soil and even time-honored laws were changed.

Of paramount importance was the Westerner's concern over obtaining, keeping and using water. The terms of his situation were simple. In the West there are over a billion acres of land of boundless fertility, yet the irregular rainfall coverage is, from the aggressive American's point of view, the result of an imbalance in nature. Sixty-five percent of the continent is subhumid or semiarid, depending upon how sensitive one is about the condition of one's country. (It is not commensurate with national pride to admit that a sizable portion of your land is close to being desert, and the brilliant John Wesley Powell nearly lost his job as head of the National Geographical survey when he was honest enough to refer to the plains as arid lands.) This shortchanging by nature was even more galling to the Westerner when he realized that the plains are extremely fertile as long as water is in good supply, as for example, in the Iowa-Illinois-Indiana region.

He would have to rely on irrigation and to create a system to transport water to where it was needed. Moreover, since the poor supply of water in the arid plains came from rivers that flowed through arid mountains to a more arid plain, it was necessary that not only agriculture but also the steadily increasing population of the plains be highly concentrated in a relatively small number of acres. Again the principle held: the towns, the cities-to-be, would have to establish themselves at the water hole—whatever form it would take.

At the outset, the nation handled this already difficult problem poorly. As Theodore Roosevelt described it:

The reclamation of arid public lands in the West was still a matter for private enterprise alone; and our magnificent river system, with its superb possibilities for public usefulness, was dealt with by the Public Government not as a unit, but as a disconnected series of pork-barrel problems, whose only real interest was in their effect on the re-election or defeat of a Congressman here and there.

Not until 1900 did the country break free from its primary concerns about water rights and navigation. It became obvious that the old riparian doctrine of water rights, which had applied in the Eastern part of the country—with its even rainfall pattern—could not apply to the West. Consequently the doctrine of priority of appropriations was established, a concept of water rights that had been used by the Babylonians, the Egyptians, the Romans, the Spanish Americans and the Indians of our own Southwest. Instead of giving water rights to landowners whose property abutted a river or stream, the priority principle established rights according to the sequence of their actual recording.

The constant battle to bring available water to where it is needed has resulted in the development of an impressive irrigation network throughout the West. The early years of this development illustrated the inadequacy of private enterprise to meet at least some of our vital national needs. From 1887 to 1893, an irrigation boom attracted private capital to the West, but the excitement collapsed and the financial backing quickly disappeared. Thus the West, which was populated by die-hard individualists, sensibly looked to the federal government for help. The government at first tried to make irrigation an attractive and profitable responsibility of the states, but the states failed to take up the offer. At the turn of the century, the federal government assumed the responsibility itself.

Congress passed the Reclamation Act of 1902, which marked a turning point in water conservation. This new law authorized subsidization of irrigation projects from the proceeds received from the sale of public lands. In 1906, the first major project was begun, the Roosevelt Dam on the Salt River in the desert mountains east of Phoenix, Arizona, and many irrigation canals were built during those early years.

Believing that the time had come "for merging local projects and uses of the inland waters in a comprehensive plan designed for the benefit of the entire country," Theodore Roosevelt in 1907 appointed an Inland Waterways Commission, which he directed to study multiple-use river development programs for flood control, irrigation, navigation and generation of electricity. The commission's first report emphasized the important interrelationship between water, soil, forests, transportation and electric power. Through its work and other projects and studies that followed, the commission was instrumental in making our deep concern over the supply and use of water a force for new ideas in ecological terms. Such thinking came none too soon, for in our hurry to expand and build we were wreaking havoc with our supposedly inexhaustible resources.

The desperate need for water and the vehemence of the litigation resulting from the inadequacy of our present water laws indicate that the nation will need to see all our water as public property. Questions of legal ownership will have to be subordinated to concern about the quality of the water itself, about regional hydrologic cycles and the effects of man's industry upon them. Earlier in this century, Justice Oliver Wendell Holmes struck the keynote when he wrote, "A river is more than an amenity, it is a treasure. It offers a necessity of life that must be rationed among those who have power over it."

CALIFORNIA STATE WATER PROJECT
1 Upper Feather River Reservoirs
2 Oroville Dam
3 Delta
4 North Bay Aqueduct
5 South Bay Aqueduct
6 San Luis Unit (Joint with U.S.)
7 California Aqueduct
8 Coastal Branch
9 Pyramid Dam
10 Castaic Dam
11 Cedar Springs Dam
12 Perris Dam

The California Department of Water Resources is in the midst of one of the largest water development programs ever undertaken—design, construction and operation of the State Water Project.

The main problem in California is that nature has not provided the right amount of water in the right places at the right times. More than 70 percent of our water originates in the northern third of the State, while 77 percent of the need is in the southern two-thirds.

The State Water Project will transport conserved Northern California water to southern areas of need.

The Project will provide water service; flood, salinity and drainage control; power; recreational opportunities and fish and wildlife enhancement.

Project water deliveries will reach areas from Plumas County south to Mexico, and from the Pacific Coast eastward almost to Nevada.

In 1968, the Department will complete construction work for water delivery to counties in the San Joaquin Valley. In 1971 water deliveries will be made to Los Angeles County and in 1972 to San Bernardino and Riverside Counties.

The Project will conserve and deliver 4.2 million acre-feet of water annually to the areas of need.

Californians themselves decided to go ahead with the plan for the State Water Project at an election in November 1960, when they voted $1.75 billion in bonds to help finance the distribution of water from areas of surplus to areas of need.

Courtesy of State of California
Department of Water Resources

AREA OF VIRGIN FOREST

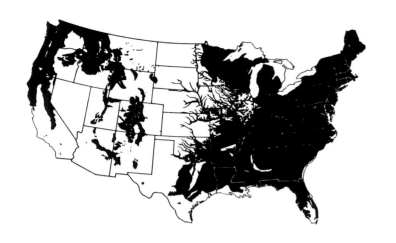

1620

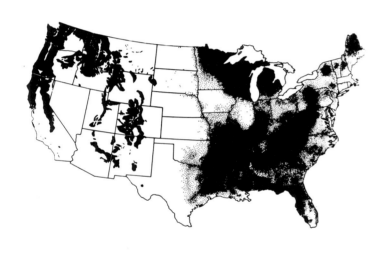

1850

1926

Each dot represents 25,000 acres
Courtesy of the Bancroft Library, University of California, Berkeley

As in the growth of our cities and towns, exploitation of our resources followed closely the development of transportation across the land. The great dense forests that de Tocqueville had seen were disappearing, their demise being traceable in the succession of boom-and-bust sawmill "capitals" whose lumber industries rose and fell, one after another, as their lust for profit consumed them: Bangor, Maine; Glens Falls, New York; Williamsport, Pennsylvania; Saginaw and Muskegon, Michigan; Marinette, Ashland, La-Crosse and Eau Claire, Wisconsin; Stillwater, Minneapolis, Cloquet, Duluth and Bemidji, Minnesota; then Portland and Bend, Oregon; Seattle, Tacoma and Spokane, Washington; Coeur d'Alene, Idaho; Eureka, California.

In New England and upper New York State, virgin-growth white pine was the primary lumbering business, with billions of logs sent to the mills each year. But beginning in 1790 and lasting for about twenty years, the primeval forests of hardwood trees were also exploited. Vast forests were cut down and burned for the production of potash to serve the British textile and glass industries.

In the Adirondacks of New York and the Green Mountains of Vermont, most of the population was involved in converting the forests into ashes. Greed and shortsightedness prevailed. Forest fires were widespread and burned deeply into the soil, ravaging the valuable organic matter and seeds needed for regrowth.

To fill the increasing demand for lumber for new houses and towns, logging pushed into the virgin forests of the Great Lakes region. By 1880, rail lines crisscrossed the Northern lakes region, aided by more than a million acres of land grants. By 1899, large portions of the great forests had been felled. Furthermore, only the straightest and best pine trees were cut; the inferior pines and other trees, such as spruce, hemlock, balsam fir, maple, birch, beech, were either destroyed by fire or left for future logging operations.

As in the East, raging fires took a heavy toll of Midwestern forests. The idea prevailed that fires were needed to help clear the land for farming and that cleared forest land makes good farming land. In 1863, 1864 and 1868, major fires destroyed forests in Wisconsin, and in 1871 the nation's worst, the Peshtigo holocaust, burned over a million acres of virgin trees.

In 1889, one company purchased 900,000 acres of virgin forest from the Northern Pacific—at $6 per acre. By 1905, this one firm alone had 1.5 million acres in the Northwest, costing it at that time close to $9.5 million. (Now the company owns 3.6 million acres, the value of which would be practically incalculable today.) The Northern Pacific itself promoted the exploitation of the forests, with the emphasis still reflecting the pioneer attitude of clearing the land for settlement. As the final stage of the railroad construction boom pushed lines through the Western mountains to the Pacific Coast, Western lumber found increasingly easy access to markets throughout the country. Shipments eastward totaled 100 million board feet in 1890 (a sixth of the United States' total lumber output). By 1898, the nation's total increased to 3 billion board feet.

Exploitation of the Western resources reflected the state of the national mind. The leading citizen was that person who obtained the biggest chunk of valuable land, and the exploiter was considered entitled to all the rewards of the kill. Under a wide-open laissez-faire philosophy, close to half the nation's virgin forest lands passed into private hands.

Since the mid-1700's, when Swedish scientist Peter Kalm expressed alarm over the destruction of our forests and the resulting dangerous soil erosion, a few lone voices had been protesting the spoilage of our woodlands. Yet, however forceful their arguments might be, they could not control the power of a new nation on the move to clear, to build and to gain profit and power.

In 1903, after forty-four days of driving and nineteen of waiting for delivery of fuel and supplies along the way, the winner of the first transcontinental auto tour chugged into San Francisco, having traveled from New York via Cleveland, Chicago, Omaha, Wyoming, Idaho and Oregon. As the railroad expansion was coming to an end and the first-time shock wave of the airplane boom was being felt, the automobile and highway-building booms were beginning to make their impact on the national life.

To repeat that story in detail, as we have the story of the early roads and the rise of the railroads, would be to tell a story of fast-moving technology causing still more rapid changes in our way of life. At the start of this century, most roads in the United States fanned out from the cities and towns to enable farmers to bring their products to market. With the introduction of the automobile, however, the general public desired to travel greater distances and at greater speeds. With the introduction of the bus, the public could travel more cheaply than by railroad. And with the introduction of the truck, shippers found that they could move their goods often with greater convenience than was offered by the railroads. New lines of desire developed, and a new combination of technology, demand for goods and quest for profit yielded millions of miles of new roads, from side streets to great interstate highways. It also yielded many millions of vehicles to travel those roads. Again, with more concern for expediency than for patience and rationality, we have thrust our streets, freeways and highways along courses that suited our immediate convenience and indicated a general lack of concern about broader effects.

This capsule history of the development of mobility in America illustrates how we have been affected by a series of eruptions to which we inadequately responded. Certainly we could not thwart such developments as the need for roads and canals, or the migration west with its need for rail transportation. Just as surely, we could not have avoided the depletion of some of our forest lands; our restlessness, our ambition and our love of profit are as much a part of our character as lava is part of a volcano. Our fault has lain in our unwillingness to comprehend these forces so as to make them properly beneficial to us.

Part of the New York State Wilderness
Preserve in the Adirondacks.

Primeval forest in California.

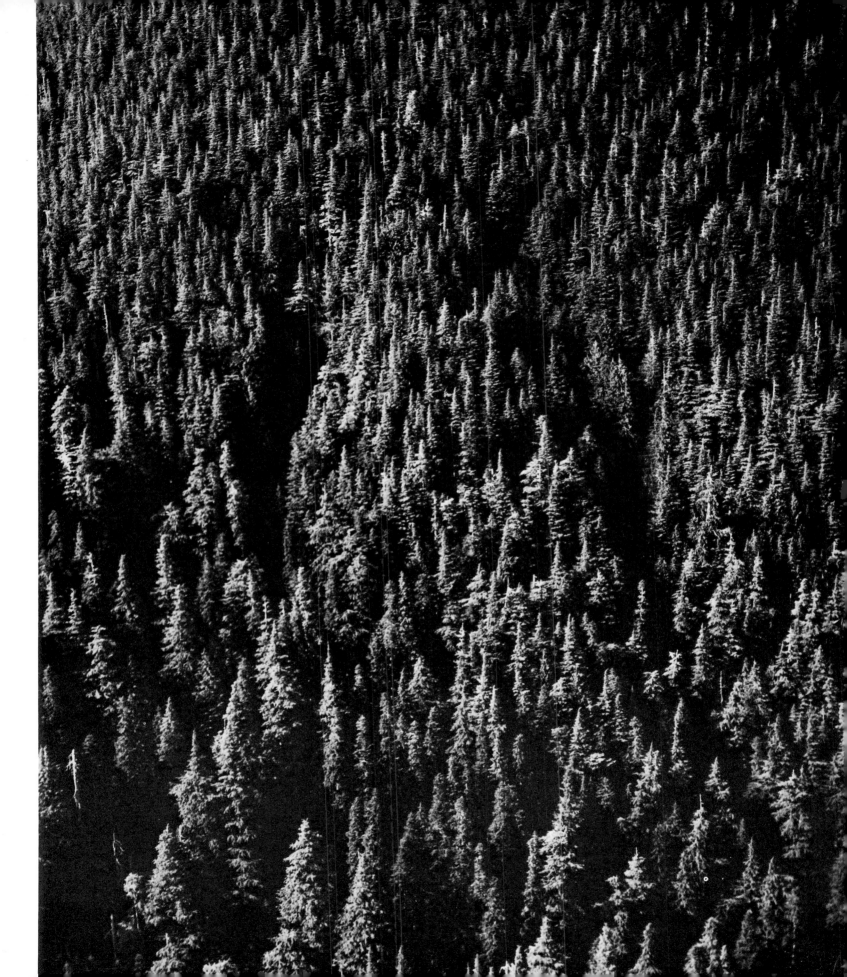

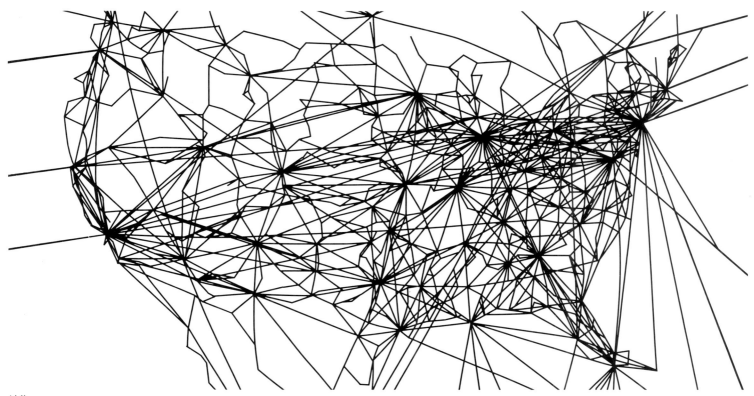

Airline map.

We are still migrants. Some of us are like nomads moving among concrete oases. Others of us are mass migrants on a phrenetic scale. The dynamics of such mobility are dramatized daily by one aspect of mass migration—that within the cities themselves. Each day, within one morning hour, 4 to 5 million people travel to Manhattan Island to work, shop and otherwise use the core city. Fifteen to twenty thousand of them may occupy a fixed point, such as an office building, stacked floor on floor and arranged desk to desk on three-fourths of an acre of land. Each day, within one evening hour, the millions move again, out of the core until their density is diluted for another day. The logistics of this mobility embraces everything from Kleenex to heavy turbines and staggers the imagination.

To see in part how it happens, let us take another look at Monument Valley. There the signature of change is not by the hand of man but by the elements. Yet what is that shimmering streak that catches the eye as one circles above the Valley? Below lie a pair of steel ribbons where a transcontinental railroad crosses, each of its silver tracks resting on a creosoted tie laid laboriously by hand a century ago; stitched with long lines of freight cars moving across the sands, the gleaming tracks stretch as far as one can see. Alongside are other traces of the means of mobility that opened up the West, from the rutted tracks of the Navajo wagons to concrete highways. And then a third dimension: long lines of silver towers rise, each like a huge spider spinning strands of wire across the land, carrying the energy extracted from coal, water, gas or oil—as someone has described it, "shipping coal by wire." Across this undeveloped no man's land they carry power from the source of its creation many miles to the consumer.

Looking still closer, one can make out signs of a lesser-known form of conveyance, the pipeline. It is remarkable how relatively unscarred this mode of transport leaves the land—not much more than a small cluster of bright steel houses lined up with precision, like parts of a toy fort, with a flagpole in the center, a water tank on the side and a fungus-like stand of silver pipes stubbing up in the desert. This is a pumping station, one of many of a transcontinental system, connecting a pipeline that may be 20, or 36, or as much as 40 inches in diameter, pushing forward as much as 40 million gallons of gas and oil at a time. Seen on a map, the multiplicity of straight pipeline paths can easily be mistaken for a composite air route map. They crisscross the country. They already traverse a million miles, more than four times the distance to the moon. They have a tremendous potential as a freight carrier.

Power transmission lines, Arizona.

PIPELINE NETWORK
Pipeline network in North and Central America is more concentrated than in any other part of the world. Map shows major pipelines carrying oil, gas and products. There are many shorter lines, some used for other materials.

Pipeline complex in Texas.

The pipeline was first developed over a hundred years ago in Pennsylvania to transport kerosene to be used in lamps. This early use declined sharply when Thomas Edison invented the electric light bulb, but now the pipeline is threatening to surpass surface transportation, both land and water, as our prime mover of goods for high-density living. The pipeline holds many lessons for us as we search for ways to solve the tangled land-use problems of our high-density urban centers. There is cause for hope in the miracles that private enterprise has performed in this field, for the pipeline proves that impossible obstacles can be overcome when there is a will and when the stakes are high enough.

Over the desert, under the sea, across continents, even through the Alps, black liquid gold flows from the great oil fields of Arabia to the Western world along a pipe thoroughfare of 2,400 miles, over a yard in diameter, with quarter-inch-thick walls withstanding 100,000 pounds of pressure per square inch. This potential is seemingly unlimited, because the smooth underground flow is unaffected by weather or seasonal changes and, by the same token, leaves the environment unaffected.

Furthermore, in a time when we are troubled with the difficulties of obtaining authority over the land so as to develop its full value, pipeline construction gives us reason to hope for a way out. The Big Inch, a 1,475-mile-long pipeline from Houston, Texas, to Linden, New Jersey, required right-of-way easements involving some 17,000 owners. Wide rivers had to be crossed, and mountains and other land forms inaccessible to tractors negotiated. Builders of great pipelines like to overcome such barriers, not by bludgeoning and gouging with main force but by ingenious use of other specialized methods, including the helicopter. If our railroads and highways are like broadswords slashing through the land, the pipeline is like a flexible *épée*. Obtaining right of way from the 17,000 owners caused little trouble, for the pipeline did not noticeably disrupt their land in crossing it. At the present time, the pipeline volume is already over 20 percent of the total land freight (in terms of ton miles) carried in the United States.

From high in flight over Monument Valley, we also see the sheen and glisten of an alien body of water. A newly formed lake is held captive by gigantic Glen Canyon Dam, with deep waters fingering up the canyons, flooding the

Glen Canyon Dam, Arizona.

sculptural red rock buttes, halting the Colorado River and its tributaries (the Escalante River and the San Juan River), obliterating a full scope of time-worn terrain; the lake is now called "America's most spectacular vacationland."

Has man's tampering created a new aesthetic? The achievement is called Lake Powell after John Wesley Powell, the one-armed Illinois professor who first explored the white waters of these canyons. As Powell insisted, this land is arid, and has adjusted to its dryness. Will these channels that once raced white water through sun-baked corridors of stone ever bring Lake Powell to a sufficient level to fulfill the purpose for which it was planned?

Glen Canyon Dam, a tourniquetlike achievement in structural and hydraulic engineering, is a controversial statement of man's ability to redirect the laws of nature—to damage the entire land and water system which it now dominates—all in the name of progress.

Can the dramatic imposition of this structure, this immovable object placed in the way of a supposedly irresistible force, be justified as a development in the establishment of a new aesthetic? What are its chain reactions? Have we the scientific ability to predict them? Do we have the moral fiber to face what our calculations teach us? Do we have a political framework sound enough to rely on reality and not on special-interest pressure groups, high-priced lobbyists, their actions and demands?

Instead of contemplating only the structure that impounds it, should we not look to the source of this huge accumulation of water and should we not question man's assumption of the power to free it or not to free it into the great natural system that cries for water below? This river, now blocked, forms one of the four principal river systems of the continent, the drainage from millions of acres of land, a great harvest from rainfall, snow and the influx of tributaries. Water flowing from several states winds through Colorado's ancient canyons, suddenly to be sluiced by gravity through generators and turbines, and then released to continue on its way.

In that instant of the river's collaboration with man, many important things happen. Instant power is created in huge quantities and sent flowing through cables and wires to towns, cities and industrial complexes. It does so silently, at the speed of light, leaving no trace of pollution. Here is the consummate application of a long-established principle, the use of the water wheel to serve man. This is its justification. Does it balance the loss man suffers?

My wife and I have taken an extended trip over Lake Powell; we have flown over it, have boated on it and have camped along its shorelines. We have viewed the upper half of a dramatic and fundamental landscape cut in two.

Racing in our motorboat 200 feet above the natural bed of the Colorado, we approached Rainbow Bridge from a marina, a parking lot for boats. Walking a short distance over a simple trail, which bore signs promising to be "improved" for women wearing high heels, we found several hundred visitors picnicking under the shadow of the greatest span of rock on our continent. Two ravens had already learned the art of rifling discarded food from picnic bags.

The old overnight horseback trip to visit Rainbow Bridge is seldom made today. That rare experience, which left indelible impressions, is somehow gone. Ease of motorboat travel removes the sense of achievement and automatically lessens the appreciation. In lessening the appreciation, does it not lessen a value of the aesthetic? It is a travesty because it has become an illusion.

As things stand now, we have a clear prime source of energy: a flowing river below (when water is released from above), and sop to the uninitiated in the recreation area above. Our concern in this book is to search out the American aesthetic, not to arbitrate the morals of man. Powell himself said there would never be enough water to bring the lake to its planned level. And so it may well happen that in the future people who are better informed, wiser in the ways of water and man's subservience to it, will take the dam down.

With such facilities as highways, pipelines, power lines, railroads and air routes together, 3 or 4 hundred million people can be sustained on 1, 5, 10 or 15 percent of the land. With such density made not only possible but desirable, we can learn to develop our open space in harmony with our urban setting.

Our waterways are still major avenues of transportation. The canal systems are solidly incorporated in our basic system. The Erie Canal, for instance, is an integrated element in the Great Lakes interconnected system for carrying goods. The Illinois waterway carries the cargoes of oceangoing ships from the St. Lawrence Seaway down the Mississippi River to the Gulf of Mexico, and has made Chicago accessible to world shipping from the North and the South, without which she would not be competing successfully with our great coastal seaports.

Inland Houston stands as our third major port as the result of a 75-mile-long deep-water channel leading in from the Gulf of Mexico. Our waterways and lakes and ocean ports teem with traffic, from tugs to giant tankers, offering a silent efficient alternative for truck and train as our great core cities draw further concentrations of people.

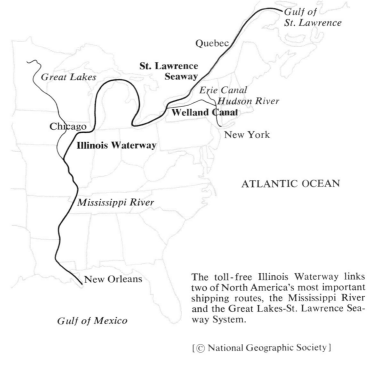

The toll-free Illinois Waterway links two of North America's most important shipping routes, the Mississippi River and the Great Lakes-St. Lawrence Seaway System.

[© National Geographic Society]

Chicago River in downtown Chicago.

Towboat on Illinois Waterway near Peoria.
[© National Geographic Society]

New cars, automobile factory, Detroit.

Mobility and place—these are our prime considerations. Whether it be the creation of an atomic power plant a few miles from Los Angeles, the building of Glen Canyon Dam a thousand miles away, the impact of a freeway system or the threat of filling San Francisco Bay for an airport extension, the historical patterns of the age-old conflict between place and mobility remain unchanged. Through the years, as we have seen, this conflict has created scars and left many of our cities uneasy trading posts, with varying degrees of damaged aesthetic values. The best that can be hoped is that some lessons will be learned before a repeat performance occurs over the building of freeways we do not need.

This brings us to what Lewis Mumford calls our love affair with the motorcar. Not only does it concern the auto, however, it also concerns a distinction between mobility and communication, two things we tend to group together. In fact, they are totally opposed in function: the final point in communication could eliminate the need for mobility and put an entirely new light on the technology of core cities. Instantaneous communication connects people and machines, machines and machines, fixed points and moving points, reducing mobility but not yet eliminating the need for it. In such a world, travel could exist for its own sake, while every service would be performed by remote control. If Norbert Weiner is to be believed, our resulting stability and leisure would offer a compelling reason for the orderly reorientation of our environment.

But this utopia seems ridiculously remote when we consider our passion for the automobile. Our car is far more than a means of transportation or a possession of personal pride. It is the keystone of our economic system, in which we, as consumers, complete the cycle of manufacturer-purchaser-consumer, to expend, dispose and renew. The production of the car affects the prosperity of a very major line of circulation in our economic system. Until other forms of transportation replace it—and they must in time do so—the auto will be the index used to measure our dollar wealth. It is the auto that is the cornerstone of the expendable-goods system. Each of us must have at least one car. We function like the hermit crab; we must carry our thousand cubic feet of auto space with us, and with it extend our linear dimensions by several feet as the car juts out around us. Since it has become so much a part of us, we have to put the creation of room for it first on our agenda. When we build a freeway, we make room for the motorcar. When we clear and destroy prime agricultural areas, we make room for another housing project that is dependent on cars.

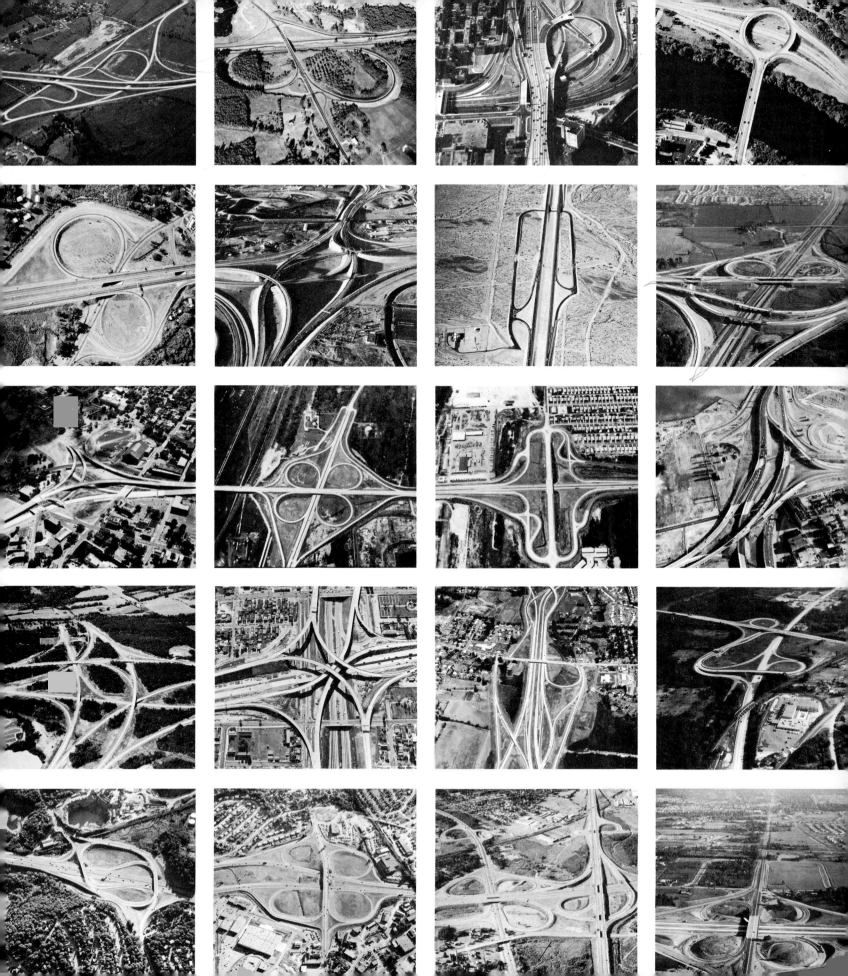

When freeways and cities are taken separately, each can be and often is a charming and aesthetically pleasing thing. Christopher Tunnard, in his *Man-made America*, has produced sensitive ideas for freeway and throughway designs and suggestions for scenic roadways that can fit snugly upon prairies and within mountain passes and gracefully cross bodies of water. We have lovely areas of Boston, New York, Baltimore, Washington and New Orleans where the confrontation between place (beautiful structures set on street patterns laid out for the horse, the mule and the burro) and mobility (the high-speed throughway) has been postponed. However, in other parts of those cities the confrontation has come inexorably through encroachments of the new industrial-technological world upon the patterns of the old agriculturally oriented ones. Of these cities, New York and Baltimore, perhaps, offer case studies of the broadest significance, for they exemplify the problems arising from high-density population and from new pressures on historic values and open space. They also sharply reflect changes in public and private attitudes.

Since the federal highway program is the mirror image of the automobile boom and has the largest public support and the richest federal purse to supply it, the most likely source of funds for combating the backlash it has brought on itself is its own grants to states. Often in the past, the grants have been used to build highways that became environmental liabilities and, in time, caused the backlash. Our hope is that we may be able to turn many of the proposed highways into assets by developing far more than one use: to provide urban public services usually lacking in the crowded areas through which these freeways are proposed to run.

Ada Louise Huxtable of the *New York Times*, a truly sensitive critic of the urban scene, has written at length about such an attempt in New York City. She observes that:

From Jefferson to Emerson to Steffens, the American City has been reviled and rejected by American intellectuals.

Those who could not afford to leave stayed, as did those who, for one mysterious reason or another, loved the cities and thrived in them, finding in their congested hearts the heady stuff of life and in their polluted air the scent of creative vitality. When the planners and the renewers came to give them light, air, open space and safe and sanitary standardized habitations, they fought them. They stopped the renewers and blocked the road builders, and in many cases they were right. But they were not all right, or right without reservation. Whatever urban values have been saved, there is no camouflaging the deterioration of urban housing, the inadequacy of urban transportation, the tragedy of the slums

and the failure of education.

This cannot be rationalized by nostalgia, rugged individualism or the mystique of some brand of modern urban romanticism. Romantic the city is, and romantic it must remain, but it is also a chamber of horrors for many. We need the schools, the housing and roads — the office buildings and industry. But we do not need them in the conventional, destructive form that has forced so many thinking and feeling citizens to the barricades. If we stop fighting long enough, we may even see that some of the things we are fighting may carry the seeds of salvation. In the super-road, the city-as-a-building may be the answer to our problems. These may be the tools that we need to use creatively.

It took the form of a proposal for Linear City to run five and a half miles on the air rights over the Cross-Brooklyn expressway. The planning proposal remains almost universally applicable to the expressway problem. The Linear City proposal grew out of a typical, tragic big-city problem. Five central Brooklyn communities are desperately in need of schools. The answer was to build the city's proposed Cross-Brooklyn expressway, as part of a larger urban design that would include the necessary schools, plus housing and community facilities. These buildings would all be constructed on the air rights above the road. The Linear City comes out of a distinguished theoretical tradition. It was proposed as early as 1910. It almost seems to be in the cards, logically and inevitably, for a civilization that must build roads, and use cars, and house and serve vastly increasing numbers of people in urban centers. You cannot outlaw the twentieth century.

But here the trouble begins.

The scheme has the backing of the Mayor, the Board of Education, the City Planning Commission and the Transportation Administrator. It is not a matter of money; there are funds for roads, capital budget allocations for schools and public works; there are ways to finance housing. It is a matter of putting the allotments together that would be used separately. Nor is a design a problem. There is plenty of talent available to develop it in proper human terms — technology, multilevel engineering know-how. The real problem is simple and appalling. In government everything is solidly stacked against getting anything done. A proposal of the scope and size of Linear City must cut across all city departments. A design breakthrough is not enough. An administrative breakthrough is equally necessary.

The procedure is standard Kafka, or Bureaucratic Nightmare. If the scheme is scuttled, it will not be for lack of vision, talent and technology, but because of the insurmountable government course that functions less for action than for its own sake. Not for a nail is the kingdom lost today, but for a kind of operational Parkinsonian-McLuhanism in which the process is the product.

The future can be defeated handily at any time in an age of the absurd. In New York, the effort to create the Linear City is real. The idea of Linear City may stimulate the imagination and courage needed to cut the Gordian knot of bureaucratic hesitation and self-serving that has tied up New York for decades. For a more promising prospect, however, let us turn to a core city that lies farther to the south.

Fort McHenry, Baltimore, Maryland.

THE REBIRTH OF A QUEEN

The people of Baltimore have always been famous for their rugged individualism. Largely because of their tendency to think for themselves, the City of Baltimore and the State of Maryland are now jointly embarking upon a large-scale experiment that may have an important effect on America's future. It is an effort very much in keeping with this city's history and spirit.

The long and eventful history of this "Queen of the Atlantic Ports," as it unfolds from earliest colonial times when Baltimore was the central city of the Crown Colony of Maryland (the second smallest of the original states), is not only a review of each stage of the development of mobility in America but also the record of a community's formation, growth and stubborn defense of its historical traditions and environmental values. From the beginning Baltimore has maintained a strong sense of place, seeing herself as a settled focus for maintaining traditional values instead of a way station. Her general attitude toward all external interference is expressed by this quote from a contemporary historian:

In the years immediately preceding the Declaration of Independence, the practice of self-government became so intensely an ideal of the people of Maryland that, on occasion, they offered resistance not only to the proprietary—the Royal Governor, the Parliament and the King, but also to what they considered the unwarrantable encroachments of the Continental Congress. In fact, the instructions to its delegates to the Continental Congress were to vote *against independence*, and were only changed when it looked as if they were the only holdout.

Baltimore lies at the head of tidewater upon the Patapsco River, one of the deep-water estuaries of Chesapeake Bay. Not only is the city situated on deep water, but within a few hundred yards of shore the land begins to rise, so that in the early years rushing streams flowed through deep ravines to provide power for flour mills, upon which the city's wealth originally depended. Today these lands are parks and pleasant residential areas.

In this first phase of Baltimore's founding and prosperous growth, she capitalized to the utmost on using the mobility of deep-water shipping. Her capacity to deliver her much-wanted flour to any port in the world, faster than anyone else, was universally renowned, for she had developed a hardy breed of seafaring men and her own model of sailing vessel, the famous Baltimore clipper, noted for its ability to sail closer to the wind than any other type of sailing craft.

Such purposefulness was reflected in still other ways. A reluctant signer of the Declaration of Independence, Maryland nevertheless proceeded to make her mark on the course of the war. As General Washington worked desperately to escape across New York's East River from the oncoming British, the famous Maryland line held against the redcoats. When the British took Philadelphia in 1776, Baltimore became the seat of the Continental Congress. In 1814 the Marylanders were just about the only ones around still fighting when the British were burning Washington. They set up a one-ship blockade and held onto Fort McHenry.

These burghers of Lord Baltimore's Crown Colony were second to none in aggressively seizing the main chance. Having successfully established Baltimore as the Queen of the Atlantic Ports, they were quick to respond when, at the time of the national canal boom, the Erie Canal in New York State endangered their supremacy in fast transport. They lost no time in taking steps to meet this threat and on February 18, 1827, a Baltimore banker held a momentous meeting, which resulted in the construction of the nation's first railroad, appropriately named the Baltimore & Ohio. There the bantam locomotive, called the *Tom Thumb*, demonstrated that steam power would serve the railroad best. Baltimoreans again found themselves in the forefront in developing the nation's means of mobility.

As a border state between the North and the South, where wheat growers and free labor dominated the economic scene and slave-owning tobacco growers maintained the socially relaxed charm of the old South, Maryland was in a position to enjoy the best of both worlds. Because of this, the famous Mason-Dixon line was anchored in this city, marking the political as well as the geographical division between North and South during the crucial years before the Civil War.

Here then is a city whose political, economic and social history embodies the glories and failures of American growth. Having given birth to the railroad and having exploited it to the fullest, Baltimore also became the railroad's victim. Both in trackage and in their contribution to the economy, the Baltimore and Ohio and the Pennsylvania railroads dramatically illustrate the type of land-use problems that must be reconciled if an aesthetically acceptable environment can be recreated in Baltimore. The lesions, scars and open wounds that have been caused—not just in Baltimore but the country over—by the nineteenth-century intrusion of the railroad into cities, pose one of the core cities' greatest unsolved renewal problems.

Baltimore has also suffered from virtually every other ill that has befallen American cities. The old city stagnated, hemmed in by a suburban population doubling its size each

decade, spreading out and consuming the surrounding cheap farm lands, causing the inevitable fallout of unplanned, chaotic growth. In 1904 a great fire in the central core destroyed much of Baltimore's old-world charm, but despite this she managed to retain a substantial part of that original quality and style that was unique to her.

It has taken tenacity and stubbornness to hold out, even partially, against pressures of saturation caused by always increasing numbers of automobiles. The nationwide federal highway program was designed to meet these demands by providing a transcontinental freeway system, but it raised more problems than it solved. In city after city along these highways, and among the communities lying between the cities, the results have been damaging. Indiscriminately, the freeways have cut through neighborhoods, parks and historic areas, repeating the pattern of unconcern about the land that began with the cutting of the colonies' first roads. Similarly, the freeways have often been as much a source of environmental wounds as were the railroads in the last century. Part of the tragedy is that the cities themselves have rushed with a strange sense of urgency to cooperate in their own mutilation. As long as the ribbons of concrete would support the cars and get them to their destinations by the shortest, fastest and—usually falsely considered—cheapest route, they were accepted. Although the federal government financed up to 90 percent of the cost of these interstate projects, it left resolving controversies over routes and other environmental decisions mostly to the respective states. Thus each snarl of freeway was in essence created by each locality agreeing, usually under pressure, to state proposals, without fully comprehending the impact of their action upon their community.

In this unequal battle, rights of way were determined often in the face of bitter protests by individuals, minority groups and sometimes whole neighborhoods. Condemnation procedures were executed and the land was cleared regardless of the consequences to historic landmarks or economic conditions, and the great concrete highways and interchanges were built willy-nilly. In time, but too late, the dazed city fathers would realize that the freeways were efficient only in off hours, that traffic jams still occurred and that much of the personality of their community was gone.

There is always much talk about the highway engineer and his role in causing alleged havoc to our environment through the freeway systems he designs. Let this statement, made in February, 1968, by Public Roads Administrator Lowell Bridwell, illustrate my point:

Let me digress for a moment on what kind of creature an engineer is. He is a physical scientist, schooled in orderly answers, exactitude, precision, and conservatism. He has become thoroughly cost-conscious by training and experience. Time after time an engineer will tell me, "It can't be done." My standard answer is, "I am very surprised. I thought engineers could do anything. Go back and look again."

The need for a "fall guy" has put the engineer in almost as bad repute as the bulldozer. In all fairness, one could not blame the engineers, when the system that employed them was at fault. Under the law, they were not authorized to inquire into the effects of the multitude of environmental changes inevitably resulting from the intrusions they designed. The focus was on the imposition of a single-purpose form of transportation upon the life of each community.

If, as a sop to the local demands for beauty, a landscape architect was called in, he was expected to hide the structure, not to shape it, to plant bushes or trees to hide it, not to change it. He was to provide the superficialities of decorations to cloak the demands of engineering efficiency. Thus at no point in the process was there an opportunity for a professional concerned with the humanities to raise fundamental issues and to ask embarrassing questions. This process seemed to produce what Wolf Von Eckardt termed "dangerously explosive agonies of displacing large numbers of families ... disrupting communities, destroying cherished views, buildings and amenities ... and jamming more automobiles into the already congested central business district."

Baltimore, too, was threatened with disruption. Historically and economically, the core of Baltimore stands against the Inner Harbor of the city. At Fells Point, the first settlements were established; at Jones Falls, the tall buildings of the central business district have risen; on Federal Hill, a historically important and beautiful residential area looking down to the harbor has been maintained. From the east section of the city, the freeway that was first proposed would have cut across Fells Point, forcing the destruction of buildings that, when renovated to their original condition, could provide excellent examples of fine Colonial and Federal-period architecture. It would then have divided into two main streams, one cutting the fringe of the central business district to link with the already built Jones Falls Expressway, which rips an unsightly gash through the center of historic Baltimore; the other stream would have crossed the Inner Harbor as a bridge and again divided in two, with one branch cutting off a side of the Federal Hill area before heading southwest and the other branch cutting north and west into the Franklin-Mulberry section, a blighted minority district of great sociological sensitivity. Then the freeway would have carved its way into scenic Leakin Park and have perforated that open space with spaghettilike swirls of concrete as it linked up with the rest of the interstate system.

Baltimore refused to agree to the alignments proposed, on the grounds that they represented bad planning and that political expediency had created an atmosphere of urgency that would accomplish unsound goals, even to the extent of developing a threat of withholding huge grants-in-aid unless the state proposals were affirmed.

Yet, every time the city of Baltimore went to the engineers for a freeway plan, such agonies seemed to loom before her. The various agencies were at loggerheads and Baltimore's long-term highway planning was in the doldrums. At this point, somehow or other, things began to happen. For one thing, the federal establishment took a new look. Sparked by resistance by such cities as Baltimore, New Orleans and San Francisco, a national revulsion against freeways developed across the nation. The reaction to this public protest in turn seemed to soften the attitudes of the Bureau of Public Roads.

No one could wish away the need for arteries of mobility, nor could rapid transit be seriously offered as a total substitute even in the central core city, or the need for a balanced transportation system, which of necessity must include freeways. The need was not at issue, but the method of supplying that need. It was suggested that one way to handle a necessary freeway system was to "do what the ancient Romans did with the aqueducts, make these roads into fine, civic monuments." Or in the words of another critic, "The goal is the creation of a new, integrated, handsome and urbane kind of freeway with which cities can live."

As Baltimore continued to hold out for creative guidance more appropriate to the needs of a human community, a great idea surfaced and took refreshingly simple form: if many considerations involving human and environmental values should go into designing lines of mobility, why not bring together professionals specifically qualified to ask the right questions and to come up with sound answers, professionals who may jointly create the right design before disruptive site determinations are made.

This idea, sponsored by Mayor Thomas D'Alesandro III, has been taken up by the City of Baltimore and the State of Maryland and the Bureau of Public Roads of the Department of Transportation, which are now launched on a large-scale experiment to make what has been euphemistically named the "Urban Design Concept Team" a working concept. Only time can tell what this Urban Design Concept Team approach will contribute to urban design or even whether it is workable. In any case, this idea has been hailed with optimism. Yet, any idea that must grow under the glaring lights of the public forum and survive the buffetings of a rugged political climate has some serious problems to overcome. The optimism could turn out to be unwarranted.

For any chance of success to exist, substantial support from the Federal Department of Transportation and its Bureau of Public Roads, jointly with the cooperation of the city and state, has been essential and is forthcoming. The formation of the Baltimore Urban Design Concept Team marks the nation's first official approval of such a program by these agencies. Thus authorized, an operating team was brought together, promising through a broad variety of disciplines to produce good solutions to the problems haunting the City of Baltimore. The Concept Team consisted of a hard core of specialists in traffic analysis, highway engineering and urban rapid transit with the over-all coordination of these specialists charged to the architect-planner functioning in his own field, supported by consultants retained in geophysics, sociology, minority group representation, economics, implementation proceedings, acoustics, landscape and graphics, to name but a sampling. Although the official contracting agent was the Chairman of the Maryland State Roads Commission and the Director of the Department of Public Works of the City of Baltimore, everyone knew the real client was the multifaceted body politic of the numerous neighborhoods and communities lying within the city limits.

In Maryland, and particularly in the city and environs of Baltimore, the question of how to lace tubes of traffic through vital parts without unduly disturbing the living organism of the city is symptomatic of a national problem and offers a pilot-study opportunity that can be available as an example for the whole country.

This approach calls for public and private construction and action programs to be undertaken in concert all along the 23 miles of freeway corridor. The team's job is thus to arrive at a multiple-use benefit formula for highway funds. The right-of-way alignment can serve, under controlled conditions, as an instrument of basic corrective surgery and do good to the community pattern if potential locations are evaluated from that point of view.

In the case of Baltimore, an examination of the present conditions of some possible areas for a right of way shows that they are in many cases deplorable. Industrial areas are often operated out of concern only for annual net profit and

with no thought of their effect on the environment. These areas are often considered inviolable, because they provide jobs and provide a substantial tax base for the city. However, some preliminary economic studies indicate that the cost of correcting the pollution caused by this industry, which in turn has produced more slums, delinquency and crime, is equal to or greater than the cash produced by the taxes. Clearly, it would take at least as powerful an agent as a highway right of way to dislodge the cancerous growth represented by these powerful bastions of industry.

Using imagination and ingenuity, and drawing heavily on the support of government, wonders can be worked by using the highway corridor as the corrective agency. While the expense for the freeway program itself is substantial, an estimated $450 million, this sum should be considered primarily as a catalyst for inducing private and public agencies interested in housing, parks and recreation, as well as industry, to invest three or four times as much along the corridor itself. In terms of the related and collateral opportunities, the impact of this effort could be expected to send out ever-widening waves of influence throughout the city. Of course this approach is meaningless without the full involvement of all agencies of government and representatives of the private sector, supported by creative thinking and the use of many disciplines not associated with planning. Just as the diesel engine applied to the railroad came from another industry, so these problems of mobility and place must be attacked with the computer. Psychological and sociological techniques seldom before related to planning have a vital place in the programed use of these experiments.

It is hoped that guidelines, particularly in the area of overall coordination and leadership, will be developed for the future. Since it is in this area that most programs launched today have failed, the leadership of the architect-planner, as indicated in the case of the Baltimore project, is intended to guarantee full representation of those concerned with matters other than engineering. It is intended that the architect-planner will take the role of "Defender of the Environment" on a continuing basis. As the Urban Concept Team philosophy unfolds, it may "catch on" and become the mode of leadership for enhancing the quality of our environment, adopted by the duly elected representatives of the people themselves, or by deputies such as mayors and city councils.

This job, of course, cannot be done in a vacuum. The scene is, in fact, somewhat reminiscent of the form of classic Greek drama, with its division into main characters and chorus; the City of Baltimore is analogous to the protagonist, while the chorus is made up of elected public officials at all levels of government, plus an equal number of duly appointed official technical experts, each representing his own level of county, state and federal responsibility. The theme of this drama consists of a successful confrontation of heretofore bypassed or swept-under-the-rug issues: racial feelings, the existence of ghettos, the quality of housing and the integrity of ethnic groups.

This kind of thinking requires tapping a broad variety of resources and studying the actions and reactions of typical communities on a nationwide basis. This program also called for national leadership. I believe that history will show that Mrs. Lyndon Johnson provided the leadership that changed the political climate in Washington to being favorable to aesthetic considerations, through her personal participation in a positive program. By stressing the social and economic values of beauty, she has done much to crystallize a positive national point of view toward our environment.

There was a movement in this direction as early as September, 1963, as indicated by a memorandum issued by Rex Whitton, the Federal Highway Administrator, which detailed the following guidelines:

In the development of transportation plans it is important that full consideration be given to the possibility of utilizing these facilities to raise the standards of the urban area. Open space, parks, and recreational facilities are important environmental factors. It is becoming more and more important in our transportation planning that additional attention be given not only to the preservation and enhancement of existing open space, but also to the providing of additional open space in anticipation of future development. Similarly, conscientious attention should be given to the preservation of historical sites and buildings.

Care should be exercised in selection of locations for new transportation facilities so that neighborhoods are not disrupted. To the maximum extent possible, cutting through school districts, ethnic groups, fire stations, etc., should be avoided.

New transportation facilities should be made to blend into the natural landscape, taking advantage of scenic vistas, topography, etc. The location and design of new facilities should be such as to insure a pleasing appearance for the motorist, the pedestrian, and the nearby resident.

These instructions, and others like them, were largely ignored. Their impact, if any, was designed for its public-relations effect and had nothing to do with actually changing policies for the design or construction of freeway systems.

Baltimore's Federal Hill.

Among the reasons for failure so far has been that we have, by and large, been directing our engineers to plan and build our freeway systems with service to the vehicles they carry as the sole requirement, regardless of the costs in ruined human values caused through the destruction of the environment and the amenities erased by the right of way. With 90 percent federal financing, the freeways have tended to become luxurious and expensive. Because of the autonomous power vested in state highway commissions and their administrators over the "power of eminent domain," there has been little that an ordinary citizen could do. Our citizens' principal weapon has been the politically weak city planning commissions, whose knowledge and integrity were high, but whose power to make their findings stick was low, even though they are backed by the local press, supported by the concerted efforts of urban renewal, bolstered by the resistance of the displaced groups and subgroups in the central core.

If the federal government, in cooperation with the city, county and state, finds that the Concept Team can be constituted to provide a sufficiently Olympian view and can remain, at the same time, firmly rooted in reality, then it might provide a viable instrument that might prove the answer to the nationwide problems we have been discussing.

We have mentioned briefly the role of computers and other technological means of handling our problems. We should re-emphasize here that in the final analysis there is no substitute for man, whose brain is the most complex computer of all and who must ask the right questions and make the right decisions. As an example, we might observe what happens when a poor neighborhood is threatened with the possibility of intrusion by a freeway. Through the Concept Team we can learn the dynamics of the community's situation. We can gather information for a psychological and sociological profile that will enable us to see what the people like and dislike about their neighborhood, what they think about the freeway, what they would like us to do. We can determine what forms, what lighting, what landscaping would be architecturally right for the environment and its people. Most important, if a freeway must run into the area, we can establish not only what will be destroyed, but also what can be added in schools, parks and other facilities. In certain cases, by putting the freeway below grade, we may be able to top it with a school or a shopping complex or a recreational area. We can create links between and among the new structures and existing buildings, so as to establish a stronger community. In effect, we would create a form of Linear City in certain areas of Baltimore.

Would a bridge over the Inner Harbor of Chesapeake Bay affect the beauty of Federal Hill and Fells Point? By applying architectural, engineering, historical and sociological concepts—with a strong regard for the aesthetic quality—we may be able to tunnel the highway under the harbor, or reduce the bridge to a four-lane structure in scale with the old city, or devise a way to eliminate the need for any crossing at all; but these possibilities are still dreams.

But we are making history, and as Siegfried Giedion points out,

History is not static, but dynamic. History is not simply the repository of unchanging facts, but a process—a pattern of living and changing attitudes and interpretations. There are no absolute standards in the Arts; history cannot be touched without changing it. A closer contact with history is to carry on our lives in a wider time dimension. Present-day happenings are simply the most conspicuous sections of a continuum.

And in our own days, as proof that dreams can become reality, Baltimore's Charles Center is a superb example of the graceful handling of the kind of transition that Giedion refers to. Also, Charles Center is justly notable in its own right as an outstanding nucleus for a modern core city. What is especially interesting, however, is the spontaneous local effort through which this center was conceived and created. Tracing the history of the development gives one a sense of watching a "happening," and a sense of excitement that must have been akin to the spirit of the Periclean city-state. That same strong single-mindedness produced the glory still evident in the ruins of the Acropolis.

Yet Charles Center is almost the exception that proves the rule. With all we have said thus far have we fully explained why such supreme effort was needed and why success in achieving the aesthetic is so rare? Is it really a battle of good against evil? Surely no one actually wishes to cause the destruction of any city. Nor are those who are against freeways all good, or those for them all bad. A part of the underlying answer lies perhaps in the word "progress," the Chamber of Commerce type, which means prosperity through mass mobility.

Perhaps the most effective grounds for the rejection of many imaginative solutions to urban ills lies in the excuse that they are too expensive. It is often said that the Concept Team approach can only succeed if expense is no object, thus reducing the matter to the question of what is "expensive" and what is "priceless." There is much in Baltimore that is grimy, shabby and depressing, but we do not come

across three-hundred-year-old American towns every day, especially ones where such a substantial amount of the old has managed to survive. On the other hand, our federal freeway system is less than forty years old and is still evolving toward its ultimate form and pattern.

In considering the projected peak of the automobile traffic, we should bear in mind the rise and fall of other "dominant" types of transportation: canals, such as the Chesapeake and Ohio, George Washington's favorite dream as a solution to the prosperity of Georgetown; and the Erie Canal, which caused the creation of the Baltimore and Ohio railroad. We have seen how the demand for canals peaked and subsided, giving way to the railroads. But there is also a lesson in the fate of the huge railroad station in Washington, D.C., which was finished in 1912 as a monument to the Railroad Age and which is now empty and deserted. There are now plans for its conversion into a massive parking and visitors' center for tourist Washington.

Let us bear in mind also the present peak of air transportation and the enormous possibilities that are developing in hovering craft of all kinds, including the helicopter. Consider all our emerging new forms of transportation: hydrofoils, monorails, superfast subways. Just possibly one can see, as if by the working of natural laws, a coming decline of the automobile.

Consider that we might be destroying priceless things in deference to an automobile age that may come to an end. If this is so, the cost of preserving these irreplaceable landmarks would not be too great. By our definition of the aesthetic, there exists in the juxtaposition of Baltimore City and Chesapeake Bay an environment of irreplaceable beauty, an environment that is priceless.

Whether the new climate in government will persist remains to be seen; but the enlightened attitude toward the total environment, which is evidenced in two major new Cabinet-represented departments, Housing and Urban Development and Transportation, is very encouraging.

Furthermore, one of the greatest handicaps of bureaucracy has been arbitrary dollar limitations in freeway design, in service to the principle that the road should encompass the shortest distance between two points. The realization is spreading that dollar expense cannot be equated to pricelessness, or to irreplaceable elements, such as Federal Hill or the Inner Harbor crossing in Baltimore.

As the elements of the Concept Team work together—the traffic analysts, the highway engineers, the planner-architect coordinators, with their advisers, the trained minds in the humanities and sciences working with federal agencies that are concerned with core cities, the human environment and mobility—they may well produce a unity of knowledge and wisdom much greater than the mere sum of these separate parts. With so much to bring to bear in the effort, solutions are now possible that are sound in concept and design, and that can be accomplished for the benefit of our century and the next.

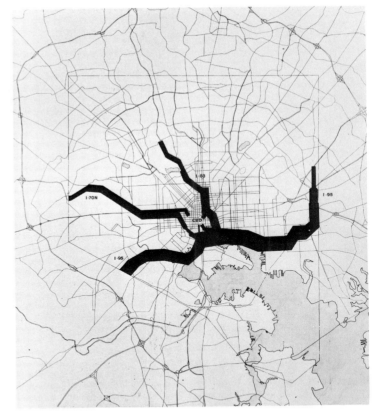

CBD (Central Business District) Service

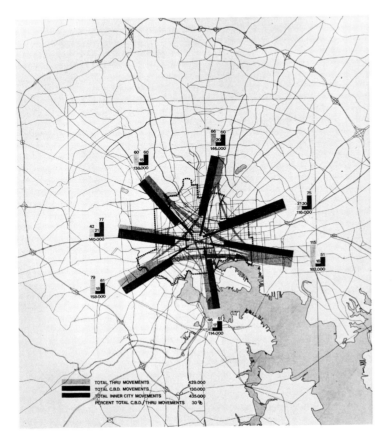

Traffic Desires (Baltimore)

CBD Service

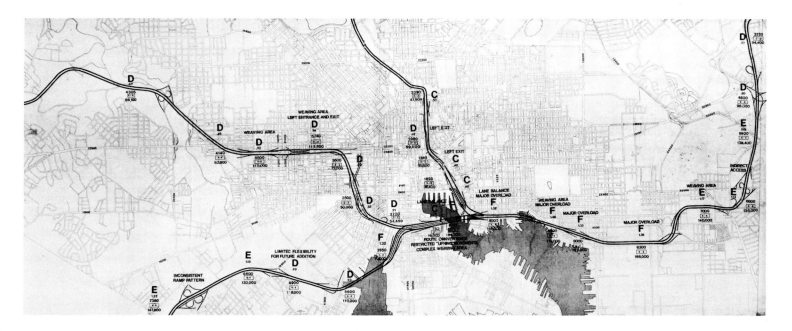

Traffic evaluation indicating the major
problem of funneling CBD and through
traffic across one harbor crossing.

A Free flow, no restrictions on desired
  speed
B Stable flow, few restrictions on
  desired speed

C Stable flow, higher volume, more
  restrictions on speed and lane
  changing

D Approaching unstable flow, little
  freedom to maneuver, condition
  tolerable for short periods

E Unstable flow, low operating speed,
  any irregularity will cause traffic to
  stop momentarily
F Forced flow, low speeds, highway
  acts as storage area, many stops

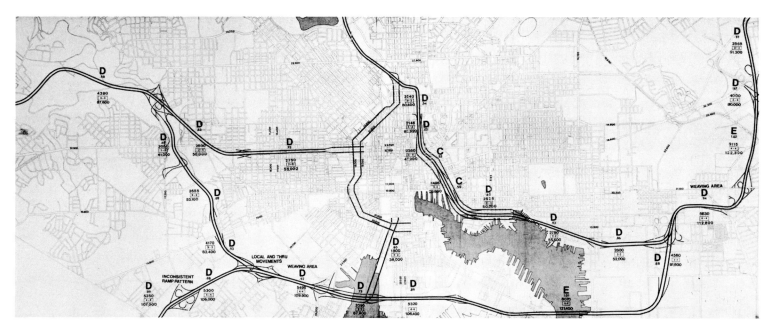

Traffic evaluation giving good service
to both CBD and through traffic while
maximizing the potential of given
corridors and minimizing environmental impact.

TOTAL POPULATION, URBAN AND RURAL, BY STATES: 1960

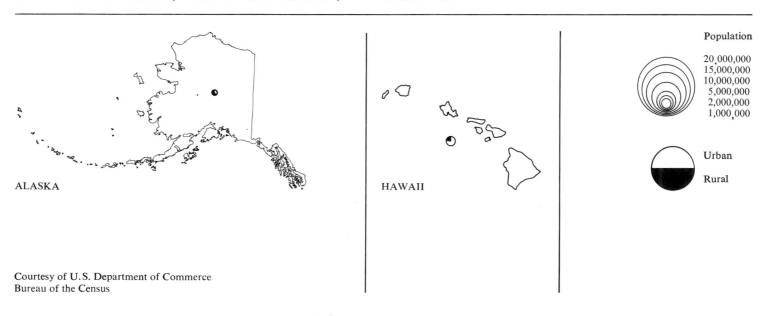

ALASKA

HAWAII

Population

20,000,000
15,000,000
10,000,000
5,000,000
2,000,000
1,000,000

Urban

Rural

Courtesy of U.S. Department of Commerce
Bureau of the Census

On November 20, 1967, the Census Bureau passed the mark of 200 million people on its census clock, which shows an increase of about four people every minute. The bureau said that in thirteen years, 1980, it will show 250 million and that that is only the beginning. Yet, to put it in the words of an expert, Robert C. Cook, president of the Population Bureau, "It is ironic to get ourselves into a population crisis in the midst of plenty of land." A fifth of the people live in either New York or California. All are oriented toward a core city. The question is can 400 million people, or twice as many as we have now, live in more or less the same metropolitan areas and stay more or less human? The answer has to be yes, and the strategy for making it possible must come in the next fifteen years. The urgency is greater than that of developing the atomic bomb in the 1940's or reaching the moon in the 1970's.

The issues, as I see them, fall into three broad areas of attack:

High-density architecture, which recognizes man's need for light, air, space and varied activities, housed in a new technology with new modes for moving about. Housing concepts such as Habitat '67 or Cumbernauld, Scotland, applying to enormous urban core areas.

Innovative design approach such as the Baltimore concept team for ordering the relationship between mobility and space.

The reapplication of man's genius and energies, which have increasingly been diverted toward passive automation, into a reorientation toward the enjoyment of man's natural environment.

What the concept-team is doing for Baltimore offers a beam of clarification, a probe in the right direction, but already there are abundant indications that we will have to probe much more deeply, and in unexplored directions, to get to the heart of the problem.

Let there be no mistake about this: for the next hundred years at least, *the* American problem will be the sickness of our cities.

Core cities—that is, masses of men more or less voluntarily gathered together to live and work, trade and worship—are older than recorded history and have always had a bad reputation. From the first, they have been objects of bitter criticism, which they have deserved. Cities do breed crime and vice. They do turn men toward violence. They do have foul sewers, dirty tenements and crowded, unwashed masses; they do nurture and spread disease. Their inhabitants, rich and poor alike, have died by tens of thousands in plagues and epidemics. Jam-packed ghettos have made them vulnerable to swift destruction, as in the monster conflagrations of London, Chicago and San Francisco. Cities pollute the air and water they live on. Their slums degrade—and contaminate. While cities shelter most of the monuments of civilization, they are also monuments to man's rapacity and cruelty. The world's great cities offer spectacles of breathtaking beauty in their palaces, plazas and boulevards, but always lurking behind the facade, stand terror, cruelty and mob rule.

Cities have not always been the core of our society. In Jefferson's day we were primarily agrarian, but now certain of our cities are gathering to themselves as much as 85 percent of the population and, in doing so, are shifting our center of balance. The five boroughs constituting New York City are presently estimated to hold 13 million people and there is no hope in sight that the seemingly hopeless crowding will cease.

The trend toward urbanization and the attendant core-city problems have not been handled on a rational basis. How could they, when no single problem has been defined? Amorphous crises tied up with passions concerning race, property rights and the public welfare have turned city government into a phantasmagoria of jurisdictions. Lewis Mumford describes our feeble response to urbanization in these terms:

The important thing to recognize about this whole process is that although rapid transportation and instant communication have altered the scale of urban development they have not so far altered the pattern. This whole vast change has in fact been taking place within an obsolete urban framework. Rapid technological advances in pursuit of obsolete or humanity's primitive goals—this is the very nature of the final stage of megalopolitan disintegration, as visible in its day-to-day city planning as in its ultimate plans for atomic, bacterial, and chemical genocide.

He goes on to point out that

The internal problems of the metropolis and its subsidiary areas are reflections of a whole civilization geared to expansion by strictly rational and scientific means for purposes that have become progressively more empty and trivial, more infantile and primitive, more barbarous and massively irrational.

It would seem that there are no wise solutions short of tearing it all down and starting over.

Each city, in whatever shape it may be, is part of a complex national fabric, and has survived so far because it has been needed where it is. Our artificial so-called New Towns, which look so promising in their newness, may have to grasp at ways to survive. The strength of any natural city is that it directly fills vital needs of those who use it. Furthermore, in his thousands of years of groping toward civilization, man has learned about himself that it is his spirit that he must design and plan for much more than for his animal wants. Inside plumbing and electric lights are not enough.

Surprisingly, our great cities—even such giants as Chicago and New York (and of note here is the fact that the second largest city of New York State is Buffalo, which has a static 670,000 in population, a spectacular drop from the 13 million in New York City)—are still in their infancy. They are actually makeshift.

Man is two things at once. On the one hand, he is gregarious and desires to live with his fellow man. On the other, he has strong ties with the soil and must keep in touch with nature to maintain his sanity and nurture his soul. Intuitively, man seeks both open space and high-density living. Sharply defined, the city must stand in the clean, clear air of the open country around it.

How basic this trait is can be seen in the ruins of the Pueblo cities—high-density, multistory, core cities—that were occupied not long after the birth of Christ and reached their highest point from about A.D. 700 to 1200. Some accommodated as many as 10,000 people. Around these great apartment houses stretched agricultural and hunting reserves. Had they wished to, these native Americans could have spread out into open country to build single-story, single-family dwellings such as mark our suburbs. Close, cooperative city living, which also offered protection from enemies—with open space nearby—was their choice.

We modern Americans have done the same, although with differences. In the last half-century, the development of our economy and technology has led us to gather in beehivelike cities, which occupy about 2 percent of the land. We, too, are surrounded by large areas of open space, in which only 15 percent of the people are now living and fewer still will be in the years to come. But what damage those few can do so easily to so much!

Historically, human density has been determined by the geographical, economic and, sometimes, political factors dominating each society. For at least five thousand years, civilization has been characterized by two types of settlement, the farm village and the city. Because until recently man's pursuits were largely agricultural, cities were inhabited by a small minority of the population—generally about 15 percent—while the many farm villages sheltered

the great majority of people. The city tended to be the home of the ruling elite—the religious, political, military and commercial leaders—who drew their subsistence and power from the work of the villagers by collecting tithes, taxes and rent. Great leaders built castles and homes in the country, but their eyes were usually turned to the cities, where their political power was most effectively employed.

This system was generally regarded as proper to a civilized world. By the end of the eighteenth century, however, under the impetus of commercial expansion, the cities had already become more dense. The Industrial Revolution and the spread of democratic thought dramatically reversed the old pattern. By the mid-nineteenth century, new machines led to the building of factories, which often were gathered about population centers. To serve the machines came great numbers of workers, whose labor became specialized. Workers occupied the urban centers, leaving their villages behind to wither and die. As their skills became specialized, new patterns of interchanging goods and services were developed. A spiral of energetic productivity and consumption resulted. First, there was a shift of the labor force from the primary industry of raw-material production to the ultimate industry of services. Basic functions, such as the farmer's production of his own motive power (work animals) and fuel (hay and oats), died out.

Cliff Palace, Mesa Verde National Park,
Colorado. [National Park Service]

Hollywood Hills with San Fernando Valley in the background.

A Hopi mesa pueblo in Walpi, Arizona.

As one flies along the East Coast today, he can observe a still newer urban phenomenon, called by the famed British planner Sir Patrick Geddes "conurbation." Conurbation is like a giant coral-like organism pushing its branches in interlocking fashion, forming a continuous pattern over the land between existing towns, villages and cities. In the twentieth century we will see this conurbation extending from the Charles River in Boston to the Potomac in Virginia, embracing a population equal to that of the United Kingdom and forming a gigantic megalopolis.

This, of course, is what is happening along the shorelines of our oceans and Great Lakes. On the West Coast, the tendrils that will become the Pacific conurbation are reaching at a high rate of acceleration from San Diego northward through Los Angeles to Santa Barbara, spreading even into the parched desert. At the base of the Great Lakes, we find an enormous hub forming, with Chicago and Detroit as the principal core cities but encompassing Omaha on the west and Buffalo on the east.

Conurbation represents a powerful counterforce to our efforts to design efficient and pleasant cities. The land is being chopped into thousands of temporarily usable fragments, stripped of its natural contours and covered by the suburban population fallout. This is created by a spiral of mutual encouragement and growth between the cities' business needs and suburban housing speculation. Furthermore, by making our core cities unlivable we have helped make conurbia inevitable.

Conurbation is no alternative to the civilized megalopolis. It lacks the means to stabilize our daily communications between high-density living areas and expansive open and recreational space. As the megalopolis stretches across traditional political boundaries, it reveals how obsolete are our divisions of state, county and city. In the New York City area, which actually encompasses part of New Jersey, New York State and Connecticut, the need for regional governments has resulted in "tri-state authorities," set up to handle problems of transportation, supply, zoning and taxation.

These makeshift innovations, however, are only clues to the most basic revision needed. We are sorely burdened by obsolescence in our democratic form of government, our institutions and our philosophies, all of which should be fresh and modern.

For all its careful separation of political powers, executive, legislative and judicial, together with the two-party system, our democracy seems to provide no workable system of checks and balances regarding specifically what we do about our environment. Although we might be reminded that we have plenty of checks—too many of them—we still do not seem to understand the laws of cause and effect as they influence our environment. We tend to emphasize urgency and expediency in getting things done. We are proud to the point of arrogance about our talent for change, unplanned change, motivated by the myth that change is progress. Looking through the polluted air, we see this constant change: freeways half-completed, oceans of subdivisions still taking shape, great industrial complexes under construction. We see brutal demolitions of entire urban entities, leaving a void that we individually or collectively as a people, guided by obsolete goals, obsolete ideas, obsolete methods of governing ourselves, are incapable of filling with something better. We helplessly continue to build an obsolete world.

The obsolescence begins with our concept of land tenure; we cling to the antiquated concept that man, with a life-span of seventy-five years, can work his will upon the land forever, with no obligation to his heirs or the commonwealth. Land tenure and the single building—the isolated structure —located on a separate piece of land owned in fee simple: this has been the cornerstone of land development throughout our nation's history. We hold to this principle even when proof of its inadequacy in the modern world confronts us from city to city. We lament the pangs of urban sickness but refuse to attack the major cause of the malady.

Regard suburbia. Rank upon rank of single-family dwellings stretch across the land. From the air they look like rows of boxes locked in place by streets running straight and endless or enclosed by swirling curlicues. One could get lost down there—and many people do. Surely, one thinks, I am deceived by the angle of view. These worm's tracks were not meant to be seen from above. At street level, they must be handsome. Yet at street level the monotony is emphasized even more. Except for minor differences—a slightly different porch, or a variation in the color of a door or a bush planted here instead of there—the houses look the same not only on the outside but on the inside as well. Supposedly, the millions who have "escaped" to these tracts sought freedom from the regimentation of the cities; they sought their little piece of land on which to be individual and original according to their own tastes. In reality, the sameness of these projects has taken them over. Surrounded by houses almost identical with their own, surrounded by people whose status, economic range, education, background, opinions are the same as their own, these people, like chameleons, have adopted the coloration of their surroundings. They furnish their homes much the same as those of their neighbors, because they buy mass-produced products from the same mar-

ket. Their recreation is much the same. Their children grow up to be alike. They think of themselves as individualists, but in truth do they not seek the conformity that we call appalling? To attain the illusion of individualism they have taken on the responsibilities of maintaining poorly designed, poorly built, mass-produced houses, which are heavily mortgaged. Pursuing the American dream of every man having at least his little plot of ground with his cottage upon it under his patch of sky, he soon discovers that his house may be little more than a few feet on either side from that of his neighbor. He discovers that the privacy he wanted so badly in the city is not easy to preserve in "the country." Having dreamed of a place from which he could look upon broad vistas bathed in birdsong or gentle silence, a place where he could sink roots into life-giving soil for himself and his descendants, *Homo suburbianus* awakes to find that he has been taken. He is trapped — there is no escape and they have even cut down the trees! The air is thick with the sounds and smells of his own and his neighbors' autos and power lawnmowers, and with smog and dust, which supposedly had been left behind in the city. With these trials also comes the realization that people can become one with a homestead but not with a tract. Impersonal, drab sameness offers stony soil and withers personal roots.

Top, left to right:
Multiple dwelling, Santa Monica, California.

Housing, Lakewood, California.

Housing, San Francisco, California.

Bottom, left to right:
Housing, Sunset District, San Francisco, California.

Housing, Palo Alto, California.

Multiple dwellings near Long Beach, California.

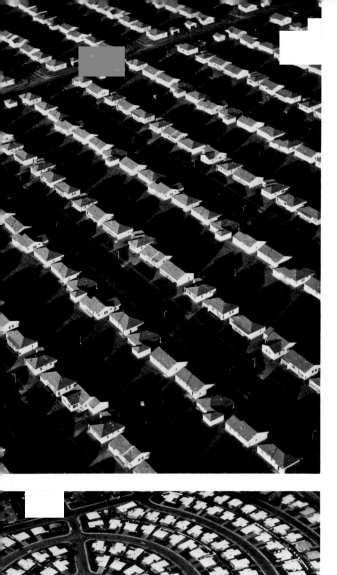

San Francisco sprawl, with part of Oakland and Berkeley across the bay.

Based on an obsolete type of land tenure, suburbia is the product of the Jeffersonian agrarian ideal of the single-family house as every man's castle. Even today it is apparent that suburbia lacks the essential nerve center of community relationships. Instead it is the result of a financing and credit system oriented toward the developer rather than the community. Pursuing the American dream, suburban man has no choice but to accept the inconveniences and fatigue of having to travel great distances, at great loss of time, between his dwelling and his place of work. Because the projects sprawl over great tracts of land, the grocery market around the corner has been replaced by the shopping center many blocks away, making necessary the added expense of at least one extra automobile. To attend the opera, theatre or symphony in the core city is expensive and time-consuming even if the suburbanite were motivated in that direction, which most are not, so he lives his good life before the Westerns on television and the hamburgers on the barbecue grill.

Solutions to this cycle involve the re-establishment of high-density, stratified, multiuse of land to produce compact and efficient communities. This means the abandonment of single-family land tenure and the development of a use concept treating the land as a public trust, a national resource — owned, planned and developed to reduce travel and reintroduce community life.

Take a lesson from the British, who limit freehold property rights and encourage long-term leases with restrictions, and thus have succeeded in keeping many parts of London charming. Cities can no longer exist as conglomerations of separate and independent units and be healthy.

Communities are composed of space and individuals. The best interests of the individuals lie in shaping the space in accordance with environmental balance. This means stratification, so that a variety of functions (such as transportation, including vehicle storage, both light and heavy; and basically residential usage, including education, worship, public gardens and recreation and community service) take place on the same basic unit of land. A city must contain a complete inventory of organic parts, which together create an organic unit. From age to age the names vary, but always a city must have a market place, a cultural center and residential areas, with collecting-places for mass spectacle and expression — religious, political and artistic. To survive, a city must also have continuity and historical awareness and an educational tradition ensuring the continuation of its development. It must also be a natural crossroads of commerce and industry. A city is an organic thing with a personality of its own. Significantly, with the exception of a very few cities

such as Washington and Indianapolis, our cities were unplanned, developing with varying degrees of spontaneity and evolving functionally. Under this heading come Boston, New York, Philadelphia, Pittsburgh, Baltimore, Portland, Seattle and San Francisco; New Orleans, St. Louis and Kansas City, their faces to the Mississippi River and their outlook to the West; Salt Lake City and Denver, posed as gateways to the Rockies; Chicago, Buffalo, Toledo and Cleveland, located on the Great Lakes. Our community cities survive and grow because they are indispensable. They automatically create the places one wants to go, or provide rapid access to them. For New York, Manhattan provides ideal central-city facilities; they are not far from residential areas and are in the center of the city itself. Good stores or theatres may be a short subway or cab ride away. The principle of convenience harks back to the New England townsite and the Indian pueblo, both of which were so surprisingly comfortable and efficient. Modern stratification of functions can accomplish the same thing.

Los Angeles, a transitional phenomenon (although called by many the city of the future) with no form or boundaries except the Pacific Ocean, is no city at all, but a loosely knit series of single-family tract houses dependent on private car for mobility, since the density is too low for either bus or rapid transit. At the heart of a concentration of 9 million people, Los Angeles will, by the year 2000, experience a total change of physical form on her existing site. Los Angeles is not alone as a product of hasty innovation.

Since the bulk of our land was taken over by the government before it was occupied by settlers, the public domain is the largest single tenure in the United States; over half the country west of the 100th meridian is in public ownership. Consequently, Congress has set up agencies and passed laws affecting land tenure. Tackling piecemeal each problem that arose, it has created housing agencies and finance agencies to control environmental development. As architect of the land-use policies over the years, Congress has managed the country's rarest assets disastrously, with the single exception of the national forests under the Departments of Agriculture, National Parks and the Interior. Each special-interest group — the farmer, the miner, the homeowner, the war veteran, the motorist — has been treated as a special client and has received solutions tailored to its need. Farm subsidies, FHA loans, homesteading, use of national forest land, water and irrigation control, together with the use of gas taxes for highway systems — these measures and many others represent a conglomeration of conflicting and often harmful laws. Probably in no other field are amateurs allowed to function so decisively on vital issues, yet in problems that affect the fate of our environment—our very survival—we, through our government, permit just that. Clearly we cannot hope to solve the problem of the cities by continuing such amateur improvisation.

Our English forebears were wiser than we, and better understood the practice of land abuse. They set up two obstacles to the fragmentation of the land: the laws of primogeniture and entailment—both of which directed the inheritance of undivided property. Behind this was an effort to keep land in trusteeship rather than as a commodity for sale. We need still more effective instruments. We must see our land as a totality. Government is ripe for legislation embodying the recognition of beauty and conservation as vital economic factors. It is ripe for constructive legislation permitting radical new concepts of the use tax and money credits in kind, in the form of natural resources themselves.

Evidence of an awareness by the American businessman of the environment as a creative tool is beginning to show.

Los Angeles sprawl.

In downtown Manhattan, the street plan of the Wall Street area has been unchanged since the days of the first Dutch colonial settlements. Over the years, winding cow paths became streets. Building after building rose, crowding one upon the other, until the only open space in those shadowed chasms was the graveyard of Trinity Church. The gloom foreshadowed crisis. Was the world's greatest financial district going to pull up stakes and flee north to midtown in search of space and sunlight? Would the concentration of wealth, power and activity manifested in the horde of towering buildings strangle an area that it had made proud and famous? If this movement was to be stopped, major environmental planning and pioneering had to be done.

David Rockefeller and the Chase Manhattan Bank led the way, but, understandably, only after Mr. Rockefeller became convinced that the proposed plan would be both aesthetically rewarding and financially profitable. That he should insist on profit, even in the face of such a crisis, was proper, for the ultimate rewards of an aesthetically sound design must rest on a solid economic foundation. To rescue the economic security of this area required an aesthetically bold concept: a sheer sixty-story tower rising dramatically from a great square literally carved out of the canyons of Wall Street. This plan expressed a law that is basic to core cities —that there must be focal points created by open space (usually referred to as a square, a commons, a place). Mr. Rockefeller recognized that the newly created plaza of 100,000 square feet was a sound investment, since the space below the plaza of some 500,000 square feet would be used to square the economic balance sheet for the open plaza above. Today the plaza, with its massed trees, Noguchi sculpture and reflecting pools, has not only created a sense of place and contributed to the dignity of people who work in its vicinity but has also assured the economic stability of the area. This rearrangement of space, this act of faith, announced that the financial district would stay right there.

The great buildings and structures of our time *are* acts of faith, the cathedrals of our age. As eloquently as any church or temple, they testify to man's potential greatness. It is good that they are built in the service of a viable economic system. If their form, placement and dimensional concept promise to give us lasting pleasure, then these structures may serve both our aesthetic needs and our commercial heritage. Nor do they require any commercial identification. Electric signs are an invasion of the public domain and an affront to the dignity of American business, and are as out of place as would be an electric sign on the Cathedral of Chartres.

Chase Manhattan Bank, New York City, emphasis on open space in the plaza.

Our buildings and open spaces should be provocative to see and use; they should reflect how capable of gaiety we are. Considering that it's our life, our city and our money, why should we not participate personally in the pride, and downright job of creating our own beautiful cities? There should be flowers, trees, flags, fountains—things that are emanations of joy and pride and have qualities of youthfulness. It is very much up to us to convince our young people that the pursuit of the American aesthetic is where the action is.

Fortunately for us, today's youth are not satisfied with mere exhortations from us to go out and win the game of life, especially since we seem either to have lost it or at least to have messed things up. To our words of encouragement to make a new and better world (words usually accompanied by a warm handshake and a sincere look through misted eyes), our youth are looking right back at us with clear eyes and answering with irreverent requests for more help than rhetoric. As did Adlai Stevenson, they understand that rhetoric is not action, and that "being not only the governing, but the governed as well, makes the task of reform or self-discipline more difficult in a democracy." So when we talk about improving our method of government and of adopting a "discipline" through which to establish the vital balance between the utilitarian and the aesthetic, we should also provide our young people with some concrete information about the nature of our problems, how we got this way, what we want to accomplish and what real tools are available. If we subject ourselves to the discipline of finding the answers to these questions, we have taken the first long step to a solution.

So let us take a concrete example of a core city with a big problem, and see how that problem developed and what specifically can be done to solve it. Let us look at central Chicago and its severe case of railroad blight.

Just as flying over Yucatán, New Mexico and Arizona has opened to us the record of the works and days of prehistoric urbanized Americans, so does circling in the landing pattern over the Chicago area reveal a panorama of the errors and opportunities to be found amid the clutter of many American cities.

We must circle because there are six other jetliners ahead of us. Stacked high above us are more arriving planes, all part of a seemingly unending stream of aircraft landing at a peak rate of over fifty every five minutes.

In the century or so of its amazing growth, Chicago has been transformed again and again by changes in transportation. Beginning as a canal connection from the Great Lakes to the Mississippi River, Chicago quickly became what Carl Sandburg called a "player with railroads and the nation's freight handler." By the beginning of this century, it seemed as if all the railroads in the country led here, the center of an enormous commercial empire. The automobile and the truck made their inroads, and finally, as energetically as had the railroad, came the airplane.

One commercial airport—Midway—soon was too small. O'Hare Field developed into the second-largest air terminal in the nation. But this was still not enough, as our circling in the slowly unraveling pattern testifies. Chicago's men of government—its mayor and council—its men of business, commerce and industry have had to move fast just to stay in step with the pace of the twentieth century. For them the race has been profitable, yet not without cost that the city as a whole can ill afford.

Turning westward again, in from Lake Michigan, on our slow descent, we can see a great wide gash within Chicago's central core. It is reminiscent of the erosion of the Southwestern desert, but this is man-made and ugly. On this rare clear day, we can see it sharply defined—a great steel pitchfork spanning a half mile from tine to tine. Its handle lies on a North-South axis, thrust firmly into the core. The Loop, Chicago's traditional commercial center, the symbol of the might of America's heartland, is caught between the middle tines.

Below us lies tangled, rusty trackage. Two-thirds of it resembles the lower part of a great portfolio laid open, with the hinge formed by the giant East-West corridor of Congress Street. The northern part of this portfolio holds the city's large investment in real estate, merchandising, trade and commerce—one of the envies of the world. The southern part is the corroding corpse of a giant industry. Here rest the remains of the railroad empire. The dormant tracks lead into grimy sheds where once the crack Twentieth Century Limited and the Broadway Limited met the Super Chief at the railroad crossroads of the continent.

This area now lies relatively unused. Through it runs the Chicago River, spanned at every cross-street by a succession of jagged little bastille iron bridges. It, too, has been ravaged by progress.

The tracks forming the tines of a pitchfork thrust up from the handle of trackage come from the East, South and West, from steel mills, coal mines and quarries of rock and gravel, from fields of corn and wheat, and cotton and from prairies and farms teeming with cattle and sheep and hogs. Some of the track area pierces deep through the

Chicago looking north, showing massive areas devoted to transportation.

Loop, and some tracks thrust to the focal point of the city. This point, formed by the confluence of the Chicago River and Lake Michigan, is the dramatic natural meeting place of the works of nature and man.

This portion of the city is depressing, but Chicago's virility is unquestionable. It has symbolically changed its driving force from steam and the dynamo to the jet and atomic power. The great stockyards that the railroads kept filled have lost their function in our new highway, truck-decentralized economy. Yet for every industry laid low by technological change, a dozen new ones appear. The fact is that this blighted town is a "swinger" among American cities, and a cause for excitement among those who feel the vitality coming into America's ways of life and culture.

If we expect to find an American aesthetic, it should show up here where, from the first, commerce, industry and everything we associate with "typical Americans" have been epitomized. Furthermore, as we shall see, architects as vigorous as its businessmen have made Chicago synonymous with a distinctive school of American design.

Thus has American man made his impression — upon a place that seems created to receive it. Here the broad sweep of the prairie meets the great sheet of Lake Michigan: the Loop's cluster of tall structures marks the meeting point of two waves of natural mass, the land and the water.

Such elements are the matrix from which the aesthetic evolves. To see how well-disposed the landscape is to the city is to see how the city can be designed to be comfortable and harmonious with the land from which it springs. Each of our major cities is built within such a matrix.

Yet in Chicago something went wrong. The rail yard drove the city's growth northward. While this happened, the railroads, no longer having the show to themselves, had to compete with other forms of transportation. The men, the engines, the goods and the activity virtually disappeared, but the rails remained, and where they remained nothing new could happen. For decades, black smoke and soot from Illinois soft coal continued to drift over the South Shore area, dropping grime upon buildings rotting through neglect, buildings packed with people — more and more of them Negro, as the years passed — who were also languishing from society's neglect.

Chicago held America's first great World's Fair in 1893, built three great universities and was good to business, which in turn was good to Chicago. Airports were built, highways were cut across the town, the boisterous prosperity-making activity of a great city proceeded and the slums also grew. Although Chicago developed the country's first

urban-renewal project — Lake Meadows replacing famed Prairie Avenue ghettos — the slums remained, moved in closer to the central core, creating an unstable, nervous, dangerous condition.

At the nerve center of the city, Chicago's intellectual vigor erupted, taking the form of a thoroughgoing review of the environment. Rather than abandon their city for the suburbs, Chicago's leaders set out in the 1950's to create new buildings, new highways and new bridges. A great new school sprang directly from the innovative tradition of the Chicago School of Architecture, and began to change the face of the city with such buildings as the Brunswick Building and the Civic Center and the twin Marina Towers. Once again Chicago was beginning to offer city dwellers commerce, industry, living facilities and recreation — and all in one central core.

Yet, this was only a beginning. A few buildings cannot undo the damage of decades. The dreary plan of Chicago has hardly changed in a hundred and fifty years. It remains spread out in endless, pointless, dull rows of neighborhoods. There is still no dynamic center from which vitality can radiate. There is still no spatial anchor to which the outlying sections can relate. If there is a solution to the problem of urban blight in this city, it is not in scattered gems of architectural brilliance, or in the low flat expanses of the old Chicago, but in the latent power of the central core.

Looking down on this central area, we see clearly exposed the vital parts of this communal being. All that is necessary to transport people and goods and all that is necessary to sustain healthy life are available here. Yet at the heart lie the railroad yards, a great island of relatively vacant, virtually unused space. Furthermore, the yards complicate the flow of people and vehicles.

On the other hand, this wasted and ugly expanse also offers opportunity. It lies dormant — ready to respond to a creative impulse. Ironically, even incredibly, the obsolescence of the railroads can provide the basis for remaking this key portion of America.

Liabilities can become assets. When regarded as a site for multiple- (as opposed to single-) use, the space appears ample and available for the extension of the adjacent Loop's activity. The location of the site is perhaps its greatest asset in that it is near both the lakefront and the central business district.

The objective is to accommodate another central city within walking distance of the Loop without disrupting existing utilities. The area must accommodate all the uses this new community will require. Its design must alleviate the

Detail of the railroad yards south of the Chicago Loop.

transport problem rather than aggravate it. The impulse is to enhance life, not to make it unbearable, and in a manner that is only possible at the core of an enormous metropolitan area.

On this site, a core city could be built that would provide buildings for housing, commerce, light industry, business, education and recreation and a transportation and utility network that would connect these buildings. This internal network would relate buildings not only to each other but also to the larger network of the surrounding city as well.

Large numbers of people would be able to live close to the places where they shop and work, many literally within walking distance. Time would not be lost in commuting; life would be less hurried. Transportation needs would be lessened, allowing people to be in closer accord with their city. Inside and out, the architecture would establish a feeling both of spatial ease and of excitement. Far from pressing people down, or seeming merely to stack them up, these buildings would give to their occupants a sense of place, of belonging to something alive and thriving.

The design, as developed by my colleague Marc Goldstein, has been conceived as a series of horizontal stratifications that would accommodate separate but interrelated activities. The ground plan would be a table of green parkland extending from the edges of the site and running all the way to the river. Instead of being a mantle of turf and foliage covering a concrete roof, the grass, trees, bushes and flowers would be rooted in the earth itself.

An underlying geometry would order the placement of all structures on the site: a grid formed by 800-foot squares crossed by 45-degree diagonals through their corners. The design proposes two circulation networks as well as a series of individual buildings, all of these being related to the grid.

One network would lie below grade level and would be primarily for service and storage. The other network, floating above grade level, would enable people to move about the community without disrupting the parkland below. Rising above both networks would be buildings served by a series of vertical transport cores containing elevators, which would be located only at the corners of the squares or at the crossing of the diagonals. Limiting core locations to these grid points automatically achieves an end that conventional zoning and setback requirements only partially do—inclusion of light, circulation of air and preservation of view. The service system would be devoted to the circulation and storage of conventional motor vehicles, which would be able to pass through or around the site, pause at the site or park. Passing vehicles could be diverted to one of four high-

capacity routes at the perimeter, or could move directly through the site, using East-West or North-South tunnels. Vehicles that pause—taxis or delivery trucks, for example—would use a system of service streets placed in open cuts just below grade. Limited to service traffic only, these streets would connect directly with all vertical transport cores in the community. Located directly below them would be warehousing facilities. Vehicles would park in subterranean garages, five levels deep, which would extend along the entire length of the eastern and western edges of the site and which would be accessible to the upper circulation network by escalators. The garages would accommodate 47,000 cars. Like the service network below, the circulation network would be dual-level. Pedestrians would move about the lower level amid stores, personal services, theatres, restaurants—elements that have traditionally defined the edges of our streets. Frequent access would be provided to the ground plane just below and to a mini-vehicle level just above.

The mini-vehicle system, including both cars and buses, would be fully automated, so that the passenger would need only to select his destination point: that is, one of several parking areas adjacent to the vertical transport cores, or on top of gateway structures leading to the garages or at other major elements such as department stores and large theatres. Quite possibly, the mini-cars, which would serve only the core city itself, could be linked directly into the vertical transport cores. While this network would be ordered by the grid, it would not be enslaved by it. The grid would be an underlying geometrical pattern, not a literal physical form. It could be filled in, opened up, even disregarded, as conditions required. An enormous number of spatial experiences would be possible—lanes, streets, malls, terraces, courts, plazas, belvederes, hippodromes—all suggested within the grid.

Aligned with and immediately above the pedestrian-mini-car network would be terrace apartments. These would bridge the mini-car roadway and have their own street system, once again for pedestrian use only. There would be 4,000 terrace apartments, all of which would be connected by vertical transport to all levels below.

The strata above the terrace apartments would be unoccupied—a void punctuated only by the emergence of the major vertical transport cores that would support and serve the horizontal and vertical structures above. These long buildings would offer 20 million square feet of continuous clear-span loft space for light industry, serviced by heavy-duty transport cores. Their exterior walls would be enormous trusses and within the exterior structural skin, floor slabs would be hung or supported independently, allowing a

Core city site plan.

Overleaf: Cross-section perspective through the core city.

maximum of flexibility in action, such as the introduction or removal of floors as required at various levels.

While office areas would have conventional ceiling heights, manufacturing space could exceed such height if necessary. The educational facilities would be housed so as to have access to large open roofs that would serve as recaptured recreation-park and open space.

A counterpoint of residential towers interwoven among the linear occupational structures, in pairs, trios or quartets, would provide 30,000 high-rise apartment units. The same basic structural-mechanical system would prevail in all towers, imparting a sense of unity. The interiors of the high-rise transport cores in the towers would be partially devoted to mechanical, electrical and plumbing services, and partially to communal spaces. From the transport cores would be suspended structural subsystems such as walls and slabs, framing the apartments themselves. Heights of the towers would vary as well as the details of the subsystems and their attendant materials, resulting in a variety of apartment plans and fenestrations. This variety would occur within a unified frame of reference, achieving a balance between confusion and monotony.

The core-community opportunities and advantages stagger the imagination. In placing an entirely new central city in the heart of an old one, we can expand and improve existing central facilities and services such as sewage-treatment plants, power plants and police and fire departments and thus avoid the duplication that inevitably results when city dwellers move to the suburbs.

Further, the area open to commerce would increase enormously. At present there are approximately 15 million square feet of retail and commercial area in the Chicago business district. The Loop itself contains 5.7 million square feet in department-store floor area, and some 30,000 employees work in the "underroof" shopping area. In the central area of the city, more than 300,000 daytime workers are employed. And to patronize these added shops and stores would be a new concentration of people who would be able to walk to work *and* to the new and existing retail outlets. Added to this fresh grafting on an old stalk, a new prosperity would keep people in the city and attract new people. The core city would pay its own way and then some. What David Rockefeller discovered about the Chase Manhattan plaza in New York is true on a much larger scale in Chicago.

119

Research on animals and observations of men have shown that to "file people away," to block them off from a broader world, to create density without relief, is to precipitate psychic calamity, which is expressed in resentment, violence and higher death rates from various causes. We are learning, for instance, that the high rates of mortality and disease among slum populations stem not only from contagion, poor medical service and malnutrition but also from a kind of body despair. People do take on the quality of their surroundings; urban sickness quickly becomes human decrepitude. An eminent sociologist, Edward T. Hall, has recently put the problem thus:

The question we must ask ourselves is, how far can we afford to travel down the road of sensory deprivation in order to file people away? One of man's most critical needs, therefore, is for principles of designing spaces that will maintain a healthy density, a healthy interaction rate, a proper amount of involvement, and a continuing sense of ethnic identification.

We are learning that you can file people away in suburban tracts as cruelly as in slum tenements. And we are also learning that families can find room for growth and good living in well-designed apartments such as the city can best provide.

The principles Dr. Hall is talking about are being seriously studied—not as something new, for they have existed as long as men have built cities, but as something that we must apply to multiple housing as our population increases. Our object is to make available to man what nature intended him to have—a rich and full supply of sensory and intellectual stimuli. Not surprisingly, the way to do it can be found in natural first principles that our earliest forebears quickly seized upon—among them, the stratification principle.

Chicago now has a building based on that principle, a structural and organic entity, flowing with activity and virtually self-sustaining.

The John Hancock Center is the world's largest all-electric building; it contains 100 stories and has a gross floor area of approximately 2.8 million square feet. The building will have an estimated total population of 8,000 people who will live and work in it. John Hancock Center will occupy a 105,000-square-foot paved and landscaped site located on Chicago's upper Michigan Boulevard ("magnificent mile") between East Delaware Place and East Chestnut Street, two blocks north of the Water Tower. The site covers an entire block, except for the northeast corner, and is situated in the heart of the upper Michigan Boulevard commercial and hotel area and is on the fringe of the "gold coast," Chicago's exclusive residential address. It is conveniently located to public transportation and to the Outer Drive along Lake Michigan and its beaches. The building will occupy less than 50 percent of the site. The Michigan Boulevard side will feature a large, open landscape court and reflecting pool at the concourse level. The court will be connected to the Michigan Boulevard level at a grand, open staircase that will provide direct pedestrian access to the court and concourse-level commercial and restaurant facilities, and to the elevators serving the observatory on the ninety-fourth floor. The court will be comparable in size to that at Rockefeller Center in New York. The pool will be mechanically frozen for ice skating during the winter and will serve as a reflecting pool at other times.

Separate and distinct entrances will be provided for each of the principal-use divisions within the building. The Michigan Boulevard entrance and lobby will serve the office portion of the building and related commercial facilities. A battery of escalators will provide a direct connection to the main office lobby and exhibit area on the second floor and to concourse-level commercial and restaurant facilities. A separate entrance and lobby will be provided off East Delaware Place for apartment tenants. Three automatic, high-speed elevators will provide 24-second express service to the main apartment lobby area in the Sky Plaza on the forty-fourth floor. The East Chestnut Street entrance and lobby will serve the restaurant on the ninety-fifth and ninety-sixth floors and also act as a secondary entrance to the office portion of the building. Three automatic, high-speed elevators will provide 39-second express service to the restaurant on the ninety-fifth floor. (These same elevators also provide similar express service between the concourse-level and the observatory on the ninety-fourth floor. Off-peak periods permit dual-use programing.) Two shuttle elevators will provide direct connection to the office lobby on the second floor. The east (Seneca Street) entrance and motor lobby will serve those tenants and guests who use the in-building garage facilities. Truck service to the building will be provided by a ramp off Seneca Street connecting to a large loading-dock area at the concourse level below grade.

The lower portion of the building (through the fifth floor) will be devoted to retail commercial use and entrance. The major portion of the building's 300,000 square feet of commercial space will occupy this area. The next 7 floors (sixth through twelfth) will provide in-building parking for approximately 1,200 cars. The sixth floor will connect to ground

100

MECHANICAL
98th - 100th FLOORS

98
97   TELEVISION RENTAL
       97th FLOOR
96
95   RESTAURANT
       95th - 96th FLOORS
94   OBSERVATORY
       94th FLOOR
93   TELEVISION RENTAL OR APARTMENTS
       93rd FLOOR
92

91
90
89
88   E
87   11 or 12 FLOORS
86
85
84
83
82
81
80
79
78
77   D
76   10 FLOORS
75

74
73
72
71
70   APARTMENTS
69   46th - 92nd FLOORS
68
67   C
66   10 FLOORS
65
64
63
62
61
60
59
58
57   B
56   9 FLOORS
55
54
53
52
51
50
49   A
48   7 FLOORS
47
46
45   APARTMENT SKY LOBBY
44   44th - 45th FLOORS
43   MECHANICAL
42   42nd - 43rd FLOORS
41
40
39
38
37
36
35
34
33
32
31   OFFICES
30   18th - 41st FLOORS
29
28
27
26
25
24
23
22
21
20
19
18
17   MECHANICAL AND OFFICES
16   16th - 17th FLOORS
15
14   OFFICES
13   13th - 15th FLOORS
12
11
10
9   PARKING
8   6th - 12th FLOORS
7
6
5   COMMERCIAL
4   4th - 5th FLOORS
       OFFICE LOBBY AND COMMERCIAL
2   2nd FLOOR
       STREET LEVEL LOBBIES AND COMMERCIAL
       1st FLOOR

CONCOURSE
       COMMERCIAL AND SERVICES
       CONCOURSE FLOOR

Cross section, John Hancock Center.

John Hancock Center at fifty stories.
[© Ezra Stoller (ESTO)]

level by a double spiral ramp which will occupy the southeast corner of the site. Cars will be parked by attendants who will pick up and deliver at ground level. The next 29 floors (thirteenth through forty-first), ranging from 40,000 (one acre) to 30,000 square feet, will provide approximately 1 million square feet of virtually column-free office space. Local elevator service will be provided by 21 automatic, high-speed passenger elevators in 3 banks that begin at the office lobby on the second floor, and 2 service elevators that begin at the concourse-level service area. The forty-second and forty-third floors will be devoted to mechanical equipment. The sixteenth and seventeenth floors will be used in a similar capacity.

The apartment Sky Plaza, a sort of neighborhood commons or park, will occupy the forty-fourth and forty-fifth floors and will serve as the upper terminal point for the high-speed express elevators originating at the apartment street lobby. Included in the Sky Plaza will be a lobby and waiting area, commissary, specialty shops, restaurant, swimming pool, health club and other amenities for apartment tenants. The next 48 floors (forty-sixth through ninety-third) will provide about 1 million square feet of flexible apartment space. Approximately 700 prime apartments will be provided, ranging from efficiencies to 4-bedroom luxury units. Enclosed year-round-use recessed terraces will be provided for approximately a third of the units. Local elevator service will be provided by 6 automatic passenger elevators in 2 banks, and 2 service elevators, all terminating at the forty-fourth floor.

The observatory and related commercial facilities will occupy the ninety-fourth floor. It is expected that the observatory will have 1.5 million visitors annually. The ninety-fifth and ninety-sixth floors will feature a two-level gourmet restaurant. The ninety-seventh floor, and possibly a portion of the ninety-sixth floor, will serve as the nerve center for Chicago's television and communications equipment. The two antenna poles at the top of the building will accommodate all the TV stations presently allocated to Chicago. Each pole will rise 344 feet above the roof level, increasing the total height of the building above the street level to 1,449 feet. The ninety-eighth through one-hundredth floors will be devoted to mechanical equipment.

The form of the building is derived from functional and structural requirements. Office, commercial and garage uses require large, unobstructed floor areas. Residential use requires smaller floor areas and core-to-exterior wall dimensions. By combining these uses in one unified structure, certain advantages accrue in locating the residential use at the top of the building. All apartments become prime units high above street noise, with spectacular views unobstructed by adjacent buildings; elevator requirements are simplified, making it possible to share shafts; the dimensions of the building are reduced where wind loads are maximum. The tapered form that evolved satisfies these requirements functionally and aesthetically. Structurally, it has the advantage of being a more stable structure than a conventional rectilinear volume of equivalent area for its height. The tapered sides reduce the amount of "sail area" surface subject to the extreme wind pressures at the higher elevations, and provide an aerodynamic advantage not in the conventional rectilinear form.

The structural concept is similar to that of an integral rigid box, which is an optimum structural system for a structure of the height and load anticipated. It has been achieved by a system of major diagonal and horizontal beams interconnecting all exterior columns (acting in the same plane) to carry floor loads and resist wind forces. The system forms, in effect, a rigid, tubelike structure that acts as a true cantilever and not as a conventional frame. It also makes it possible for the structure to withstand wind loads without any appreciable increase in steel. Floor beams are designed only to carry gravity loads and are not affected by the height of the building, and have the added advantage of being more readily removable if two-story space is required. Interior core columns carry only gravity loads. The total result is an extremely simple and highly efficient system (less than 30 pounds of steel per square foot of floor area) for a structure of this magnitude and height. Floors will be virtually free of interior columns beyond the central core and will provide a variety of depths and sizes to accommodate the requirements of the various different occupancies. The steel structure will be clad in black aluminum accented with tinted bronze glare-reducing glass and bronze-colored aluminum window frames. The plaza at ground level, the recessed court and the first-floor base upon which the structure rests will be clad in travertine marble.

The building will be all-electric. Refrigeration requirements will be provided by a 6,000-ton plant. Seventeen electric resistance boilers at 1,600 kw. and 1,800 kw. will provide heat for the building. Forty major air systems will supply the building with 1,000,000 cfm. of ventilating air. An automatic temperature-control system will be installed to maintain the optimum space condition. The office portion of the building will be heated and air-conditioned by a perimeter induction unit system with an interior zoned reheat system. The apartment portion of the building will be heated by electrically warmed radiant ceilings and cooled by through-wall units. Primary electrical service will be extended vertically through the building in dual service at 12,000 volts to vaults located on the mechanical floors. Anticipated demand for the building is 69,000 kva. Approximately 100 foot-candles of lighting will be provided, the heat from which will offset a substantial portion of the building heat loss.

This project is a pragmatic answer in design theory — backed by the hard cash of a great company, John Hancock — to the problems of stabilizing the population of core cities. Day in and day out we fight the traffic battle, or the train battle, or the subway battle, or the bus battle, or the taxi battle. Day in and day out we stare at the cars in front of us or into the newspaper we carry on the train. Where is the freedom, where is the pleasure in all this movement? Our object therefore should be to make travel a pleasure rather than a necessity. A short walk to work is a more sensible functional activity than a long, tiring ride to work. There is an alternate theory already discussed — the low-rise high-density pueblo — also providing for walking to work. This has produced a compelling idea, so compelling, in fact, that a bright young architect is now offering a design that journalists are hailing as a new idea, even though it is thousands of years old. Moshe Safdie's Habitat, which has been on display at Expo '67 in Montreal, is the result of the most modern technology, but for all that modernity it looks and functions just like a pueblo. It is composed of some 354 steel-reinforced concrete boxes stacked in such a way as to create 158 separate apartments built according to 15 different floor plans. Inside, they are comfortable and convenient. A network of elevators and elevated sidewalks makes traveling about the project interesting in itself. The positioning of the apartments creates excellent views from each and guarantees plenty of sunlight for each. Plazas and playgrounds add to the enjoyment of the place. There is set up within Habitat a three-way system of close relationships — contact between people, appreciation of one's immediate locale and opportunity to reach toward the outside world.

In a consideration of the total environment, economy is a moral obligation. Safdie points out that the economy of "what" is an essential question. It does not mean less shelter or less quality. What we mean is the best conceivable environment for all people. Economy is still restricted by things essential to survival. Let us consider a tree. The tree has a network of branches supporting its leaves in intricate formations. Looked at out of context, the tree is an uneconomical organism. Why shouldn't all the leaves be grouped in a little box hanging on the trunk? This would result in fewer branches, less distribution, hence greater economy. But essential to the survival of the tree is the ability of its leaves to be in contact with sunlight, and therefore the formation of branches achieves this with the least possible material in the most economical way. One cannot change the criteria of survival. The presence of fashion in the environment increases directly as the environment becomes more arbitrary. Let us withdraw from the arbitrary in favor of the natural-rational. The builders of the Indian pueblo or the Mediterranean adobe village considered their environment as a total integrated organism, having to satisfy the multitude of needs which they understood in their simplest terms — the continuous versus the fragmented, the integrated versus the isolated.

How in the world of ever-increasing densities, of people living closer together, do we preserve privacy and other such amenities of the individual? How do we give each family sunlight or a view or a sense of location and a sense of place? How do we arrange houses in space without losing the amenities we wish to give them, and how do we achieve variation that also allows for true individual differentiation from house to house — an architecture that is based on mass production, in which each house differs from the other as one human face from the other. These are the problems of the contemporary city, the new problems of twentieth-century architecture, as Moshe Safdie sees them.

We answer Moshe Safdie's questions with our proposal for the great barren island, a mile long and three-quarters of a mile wide, lying ready and waiting for an ideal new town to be conceived and created for Chicago's share of the population explosion — consisting, as it does and will, of youth and immigrants.

On this now vacant land at the heart of the Loop, all the basic utilities could exist — a complete sewage-treatment plant, water-filtration plant and power plant. There can be community services (fire, police, health, schools, churches); cultural facilities (music, theatre, dance, recreation, parks, playgrounds); business facilities (industrial, commercial, hotels, restaurants, stadiums, ball parks, racetracks) — all there, and to them in this vacant space can be added a contemporary city. It would be ready-made, in segments, meeting the need as the need arises; utilizing the hundreds of millions of dollars already expended on the basic stuff that a core city is made of.

But why hasn't this already happened? Why does this project, the possibility of which is obvious to anyone who cares to see, lie untouched?

Habitat '67, Montreal, Canada.
[Moshe Safdie]

Pueblo Bonito ruins, Chaco Canyon, New Mexico.

There are two divergent reasons—both involving an inherent flaw in the private-enterprise system and the elementary law of gravity that causes things in motion to seek the course of least resistance.

First, the strong elements of the private-enterprise system are stabilized producers of raw material—finished products or dealings in finance, lending agencies like insurance companies or building-and-loan associations. Nowhere in the private sectors do we find strong, stable enterprises oriented solely to the environment, with big stakes in it. Where efforts have been made—like Zeckendorf's—the spectacular collapse has not stimulated entry into the field.

The absence of this essential element in the private sectors has forced the government to fill the breach, which it cannot do efficiently or well—as this book attempts to point out.

Why should we build in existing cities when it is easier to build subdivisions on farmland that usually surrounds the village, town or city? Because subdivisions are what is known as the "highest and best use," rezoning results and the rich soil disappears under tract houses.

There is a new public awareness that perhaps the subdivision is a liability instead of an asset; the computer shows a huge deficit to the existing environs—in fire, police, schools, sewers, water, etc.

Even more so, the "highest and best-used" jargon has a hollow sound; the highest and best use for good rich soil in great, easily tilled valleys such as the San Joaquin or the Imperial is the production of food. Our habit of trying to be all things to all countries, including our own, and our increases in population may well require the reclamation of some of our instant subdivisions back to the task of growing cereals and raising livestock.

An asset that would accompany the launching of such a project as that suggested for Chicago would be an economic condition that would no longer allow the hit-and-run subdivider to squeeze out long rows of split-level castles on land that is needed for the raising of food to feed people. But there is a second compelling reason that our plans for Chicago have more substance in controversy than in steel and glass. Strangely enough for a people on the move, that reason is a complex of fears—fear of change, fear of competition, and fear of innovation.

At the outset, therefore, there is the inertia that accompanies belief in the status quo—the vast interests, the devastating effects of the "establishment." This obstacle is epitomized by the policies of the railroad industry. This segment of the proud nineteenth-century industrial era is now reduced to a state of inaction—strangled by government regulations, powerful but unimaginative unions, built-in obsolescence, the difficulties of red tape and bureaucracy and the new competition offered by the trucking, pipeline and airline industries.

Thirty-three railroads have terminals in Chicago, the largest central railroad junction point in the world. To develop leadership and unified direction, in spite of the general corporate entanglements in rights of way, rights of territory and legalistic fascination with red tape, will require nothing less than a miracle.

The members of today's railroad management shrink from bold plans, and are reluctant to take the type of risks that were seen as challenges by the founders, who built their empires against far greater odds. There is something strange and tragic in the fact that huge public-utilities security issues are floated—running into billions of dollars annually for investment in electric power, for example—for utilities to be supplied to an urban area, but not one cent could be raised to finance the actual construction of such a large-scale urban core.

It is ironic that our system is geared to supplying, on a scientific basis, anything we need in our high-density core cities except what we need most and cannot get—new ideal core cities.

Actually, there is no limit to the amount of private enterprise that can be stimulated in core cities, since that is where people gather. To grasp the opportunities offered by investment in our cities, private corporations would do well to regard the government as a partner that can create the special legislation necessary to handle conditions obstructing development of new urban cores.

Philadelphia, where the decay of the city's major commercial area has resulted in the gravitation of patrons to shopping centers in such communities as King of Prussia, Cherry Hill and Plymouth Meeting, offers another example of what imagination and determination can do. Extensive highway and railroad systems, newspapers and radio stations, banks and offices centered in the city indicate the city's importance to the Delaware Valley region. Philadelphia is one of the busiest inland ports in the nation and handles the country's second-largest volume in foreign commerce. A growing population of nearly 4 million people lives within a 30-mile drive of what is known as Center City—Philadelphia's core. With all this vitality, should the growth of the region's economy have been accompanied, over the period 1954—1963, by a decline in total retail sales in metropolitan Philadelphia from $466 million to $419 million? During this period, Center City's share of total retail sales in metropolitan Philadelphia fell from 38 percent to 26 percent. The seriousness of the problem was underlined in 1963, when one of the key department stores in the area closed.

On the other hand, what is there about a modern shopping center that attracts people even though the variety of available goods and services may not be as great as in the heart of a great city? It is primarily that they appear to be convenient. One must drive to the shopping center, but one has a car and there are acres of parking space. All the shops are gathered in a relatively small area, and the merchandise is attractively displayed. There is less impression of crowdedness, and there is more sunlight than shadow. Going downtown seems like a project, even an ordeal; shopping centers do their best to seem cheerful. The future seems to be with them, for although they actually are not especially convenient, they offer what people think they want, and avoid what people don't want.

Philadelphia's core, on the other hand, has become inefficient and unappealing. Buses, subways and trains flow into it, but there is no logical terminal system. The existing surface transit system is basically sound, except that it lacks short-trip capacity and is not convenient to the shopping destinations people want—a crucial failing when one considers that the traditional specialization of the Center City is retailing.

There is a shortage of 1,000 parking spaces in the area, and even if drivers do eventually ferret out spots of refuge for the several tons of steel they are enslaved to, they must, as they walk, continually watch out for auto traffic, put up with auto noise, and breathe noxious auto fumes. The area is crowded and unattractive—dirty buildings block out sunlight, and one must keep moving, though at a snail's pace, because there are few places to stop and rest. One goes to Center City with the intention of getting out as soon as possible.

The remedy is to bring suburban ease to downtown shopping. Again it is a matter of turning liabilities into assets and building upon them. One such apparent liability is the smallness of the area. At present it causes crowding, but if it were used properly it could mean increased convenience. The compactness can actually make it easier to integrate all the facilities of the area—transportation, loading areas, shops, offices, pedestrian walkways—into a mutually contributing unit. Integration of plans and resources is the key. Philadelphia has been doing hard and good work toward renewing itself, so that the plan for Center City will be part of a larger

effort involving areas such as Independence Mall, Academy House and Washington Square East. The plan we are talking about is called Market Street East.

The plan proposes a sequence of seven new urban-renewal projects extending over approximately fifteen years. Not only will the projects create facilities for easier access to the area—and link existing and future transportation, shopping and office facilities with an air-conditioned sunlit pedestrian-movement system—but it will also provide rehabilitation of deficient buildings, streets and public open spaces. The key to a successful commercial area is not merely a conglomeration of goods. Rather, it is good circulation—ease of movement and rest. Potential shoppers should be occupied in noticing displays of goods, not in watching out for people who might bump into them. They should be welcomed by a well-lit scene, with attractive things to look at. Shoppers should be able to spend their energy strolling, not trudging doggedly from incoming transportation to the stores. Good circulation does not come of itself—it must be designed.

With only limited space available, how can such a thing be done? After all, if you bring trains, buses, subways and cars, not to mention trucks, right to the Market Street area, where is there room left for shops and people? Yet if you don't bring them to the area, you create conditions that drive people away. The answer again lies in stratification, piling level upon level, function upon function, service upon service. At the bottom level, forty feet below the surface of the ground, you bring in trains and trucks through a pair of tunnels, linking the accesses to already existing rail lines and truck routes. A new rail station is built on the concourse level at the Market East site, and this is linked to an already existing station at 16th Street. Meanwhile you position truck-loading bays beneath the shopping area to move the goods by a system of high-speed elevators.

The next level is a concourse, also below the street. It is an air-conditioned mall with a glass roof, so that it will in effect be a skylit pedestrian street. People coming in by subway will enter at this level. A new subway will be linked to an already existing line, and the mall will be tied in as a natural extension of the convenient subsurface concourse walkway system already in use in Penn Center. Because most people will arrive at the subway and railroad levels, communications between the two—mainly by means of escalators—will be emphasized.

The mall will combine shopping facilities and a walking avenue to area employment centers. To avoid crowding, the mall widens and increases in height at points of greatest

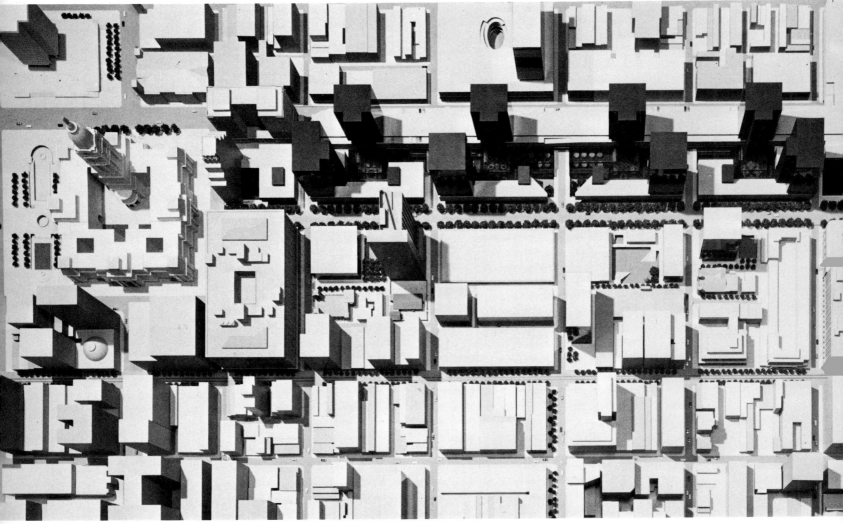

MARKET STREET TRANSPOR-
TATION-COMMERCE CENTER,
CROSS SECTION

A Market Street (Looking West)
B Pedestrian Concourse Level
C Subway Tracks
D Mid-Block Bridges Connecting
  Market Street North and South
E New Retail Shops
F Glass Roofed Pedestrian Mall Run-
  ning East and West
G Vertical Circulation Cores
H Office Towers
J Truck Tunnels and Loading Docks
K Newly Joined Commuter Railroad
  Lines and Station
L Linear Commuter Bus Terminal
M Four Parking Levels
N Open Concourse Level Plaza

Plan View of Market Street East

[Dwain Faubion]

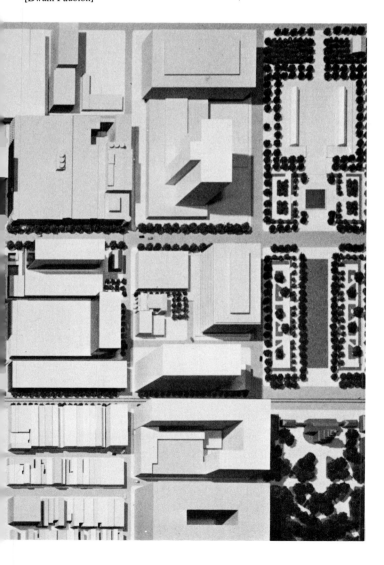

circulation. It will be divided by mid-block plazas into segments designed to meet circulation needs and to serve as gathering places, as if they were town squares, for large numbers of people. There will be shops, kiosks, restaurants and tasteful decoration. To ensure that there will be plenty of sunlight, legal restrictions will prevent buildings from being positioned to the mall's disadvantage.

The street level will be entered either by escalator from the mall below or through spacious plazas at the block corners on Market Street. They are to be protected by overhanging low office buildings immediately above. Again there will be a level for buses and above that a five-story parking facility that will create 6,350 new parking spaces, while removing 2,170 spaces from open lots and obsolete buildings —one of the major sources of urban blight.

Finally, the entire transportation-commerce center will be topped by tall office structures located to relate to elevator and service cores that will be positioned in mid-block plazas. They will therefore benefit from maximum circulation facilities without blocking sunlight from the plazas and the mall.

With its shops, restaurants, interior sculpture, ease of walking, ease of parking and a large choice of convenient transportation facilities, Market East should easily attract enough patrons to pay for itself. As we have said before, cities survive because they are needed. When they lose their purpose—or their sense of purpose—they die. Philadelphia, whatever other attractions it may have, is rooted in commercial flow. To place emphasis on renewal of the commercial core is, therefore, properly putting first things first.

Capitol, Washington, D.C.

Washington, D.C., was founded for another purpose and thus needs another approach.

Ever since the slogan "Throw the scoundrels out" was coined by the followers of Andrew Jackson, Washington has been a city watched over by transients. It is everybody's city and therefore the direct continuing concern of nobody.

As the seat of a democratically elected government, Washington is in turn governed by an ever-changing kaleidoscope of congressmen whose aims, philosophies and ambitions represent a cross-section of our fifty states. While efforts toward home rule are making headway, Congress still retains the control. The permanent citizenry are of the civil service or community services—and have only just gained the right to vote in national elections. Between the transients and the permanents, therefore, there has developed a strange mix-up of roles. Those who may soon leave govern; those who have come to stay have no say at all.

Washington is, in fact, the victim of a paradox. In their patriotic pride, Americans turn their eyes to her as the symbol of the national image. Yet those whose responsibility it is to govern the city generally look outward from the city— to their regions and constituencies, to the voters who elect them. For a hundred and seventy-five years, Washington has survived as something of a stepchild, abandoned to neglect, decay and the cruel mercies of bad architects designing pseudo-classical monster-buildings to house an endless progression of bureaucrats. The most amazing part of this is that Washington has managed to survive aesthetically at all.

The central idea of Major Pierre L'Enfant's plan of 1791, with its composition of a diagonal avenue and a tree-lined mall forming a ceremonial way between the Capitol and the White House, was long in being recognized for the great aesthetic expression that it is. For more than a century, the elegance and grandeur of the plan were lost upon the nation. This was due in large part to changes in political and aesthetic ideas. In a period of national growing up, the classical frame of mind projected in the discipline of the L'Enfant plan was swamped by the popular romanticism of Andrew Jackson's day. It is necessary to understand this inner conflict to recognize the slow working out of Washington's aesthetic inhibition—this struggle between the people's desire for the formal plan and their fear of it. This is epitomized by the anachronism of the empty Mall; it has been cow pasture, an open sewer, a railroad station, a power-plant location and the site of a conglomeration of "temporaries."

Washington and Jefferson, visiting the city now, would doubtless be bewildered and disappointed to find their monuments resting in a city marked by confusion rather than by the fulfillment of a plan that was to establish the city as the Rome of the New World. What sympathies would these men, who knew very much what they wanted, have for their descendants, who had not the slightest idea what they wanted or had?

But somehow the original plan seems to have had a life of its own, and it was rescued by planners Burnham and Olmsted through the 1901 MacMillan Commission report, which was produced in conjunction with *The Grand Scheme for Improving the Parks in the District of Columbia*. In essence, this plan reasserted the great classical quality and axial relationship of the L'Enfant plan, which was good, but its recommendation went further and proposed amplification of the pompous neoclassicism of the 1893 Chicago World's Fair, which was bad. Fortunately, the details of the plan lay dormant until the 1930's, giving time for reappraisal of the balance between the pseudo-classical buildings and the delicate romanticism of the Smithsonian Institution buildings, which are certainly the best example of this period in America.

Even the Washington Monument, one of America's finest aesthetic building achievements, is not the product of a single great creative genius, but the happy result of a comedy of errors. The original design proposed that the shaft be surrounded at its base by a grotesque Victorian colonnade. The often-hated and much-maligned Army Corps of Engineers casually moved the obelisk off-axis 40 feet and eliminated the colonnade, with the unanswerable argument that the soil conditions wouldn't permit the architect's design or location. The resultant dynamics of the off-axis shaft contributes much to the Monument's aesthetic success.

Every President and every Congress, through L'Enfant's inspiration, has had some part in the planning of this avenue and mall. We have now come full circle—to the simple but grand design of two centuries ago. It is my hope that the present plan, which I had the honor to direct (first as Chairman of President Kennedy's Council and then as Chairman of President Johnson's Commission on Pennsylvania Avenue), will provide an island of refuge, great in scale, strong in axial relationships and safe from the motorcar, where one may experience a sense of *joie de vivre* and renewed pride in this national capital. President Kennedy's original charge to the Council included the following statement:

The north side presents a scene of desolations: block after block of decayed nineteenth-century buildings, many of which are vacant above the first story, only rarely interspersed by partially successful efforts at modernization. The roadway, sidewalks, lampposts and other features of the Avenue have been sorely neglected. Increasingly, the Capitol itself is cut off from the most developed part of the city by a blighted area that is unsightly by day and empty by night.

Pennsylvania Avenue should be the great thoroughfare of the city of Washington. Instead, it remains a vast, unformed, cluttered expanse.

The central core of Washington presents in existing salvageable form many of the elements of an ideal core for any city. There are vistas and open spaces; there is the Potomac River; there is a purpose to the core, the business and image of the seat of government; above all, there are ample reasons for people to gather and linger here for exaltation of the spirit and relaxation of the body.

We have some 1,200 acres arranged into a great Mall, the result of L'Enfant's dream, with the Capitol fittingly placed on a hill; "The President's House," as L'Enfant called it, on a fine spot overlooking the Potomac; the two great buildings linked by an elegant diagonal, Pennsylvania Avenue, and all of this firmly hinged to the river. The plan was designed in 1791 to a scale convenient for a man walking or riding by horseback or carriage. But there is no solution until the automobile is dealt with. There is much loose talk, and often double-talk, about the evils of the automobile. A solution that is often heard but seldom meant is to ban the automobile. Yet are we really prepared to do such a thing? Having made it so much a part of our life and culture, are we truly about to wean ourselves of its undoubted inconveniences? The remedy is to tame it rather than ban it—even in Washington.

Our plan is to do the job gradually—first to eliminate the private motorcar from the surface of the central Mall area. This will involve the removal of four narrow lateral streets: Washington, Jefferson, Madison and Adams. The North-South cross-streets—14th, 9th and 7th—will be tunneled. Each will provide access to huge underground garages accommodating workers and tourists alike.

As the ceremonial avenue of the nation, Pennsylvania Avenue must have a noble beginning and a worthy terminus. An elegant 6-acre pool at the foot of the nation's Capitol doubles its image through reflection and enhances the unique memorial to General Ulysses S. Grant, which it embraces. At the opposite entrance of the avenue, we have projected a great national square partially framed by the beautiful Greek Revival Treasury Building and the classically correct Italian Renaissance Department of Commerce. Such a square is found in every national capital of the world except Washington. This great area, like Trafalgar Square in London or the Piazza del Popolo in Rome, will serve as the reviewing point for inaugural parades, the return of conquering heroes, and the pomp and ceremony of state funerals, as well as a central gathering place for national holiday celebrations and assemblages of tourists and sight-seers. It will form the link with the downtown business district so essential to the economic lifeblood of the central core.

The northern side of Pennsylvania Avenue will be widened by a 75-foot setback of the buildings as they are newly constructed. The avenue will be framed by a canopy of closely meshed foliage formed by three rows of trees on the north side and two rows on the south. At the midsection, this 1.2-mile promenade expands in the formalization of the historic market square. This square will be surrounded by a complex of handsome buildings including auditoriums, lecture halls and a hostelry for scholars and fellows who will attend an institute for higher education to be founded by Congress in honor of Woodrow Wilson.

All of this is part of a bigger plan designed to accommodate the inevitable dramatic increase in Washington's population, and heralds the coming of age of an American aesthetic. Fritz Gutheim, the eminent art historian, describes beautifully what we have hoped to accomplish:

Progress in executing their plans can be cited, although it may appear slow-paced. We need to appreciate this forward movement and we need to accelerate. The present generation is capable of viewing with astonishment historical photographs showing the Mall and additional park lands crowded by wartime temporary office buildings; yet these have been removed only within the past decade and some within the last year. Others—the most obstinate concrete ones from World War I—have yet to go. Designed to safeguard the continuous open space, major needed highways are underpassing the Mall. The Smithsonian's popular complex of museums—venerable, but rapidly growing—has aided in creating the newer scene of gaiety and elegance. The Department of the Interior and the National Park Service are provided the support needed to enrich the Mall as a lovely park. Under construction at the foot of the Capitol is a great reflecting basin, the first major visible sign of change in this area of the Mall since the construction of the monument to General Grant in 1923.

And he goes on to say:

Over Capitol looking west toward Lincoln Memorial, with Pennsylvania Avenue at right.

[Model photos by Dwain Faubion]

North-South axis from White House.

The Mall is seen as a new kind of park with facilities to encourage public use, to enhance accessibility, to render the Capital City more pleasing and more meaningful to visitors, and to endow this space with a vitality within its civic role. The Mall achieves a new character, but one sanctioned by the great historical composition in Paris where children play and lovers stroll in the Tuileries gardens within the royal sweep of the "Triumphal Way" that connects the Etoile and the Louvre.

In Pennsylvania Avenue another great route appears in the more formal costume of architecture, framing the life of the street and providing the background for ceremonial events of state, creating in this location the proper environment for the enjoyment of those concentrations of office workers.

And from these vital areas are increasingly excluded the heavy traffic and irrelevant activities of the city which would compromise what we mean to create here in its heart—the heart of the Nation as well as the heart of the city.

Reflecting pool at Capitol.

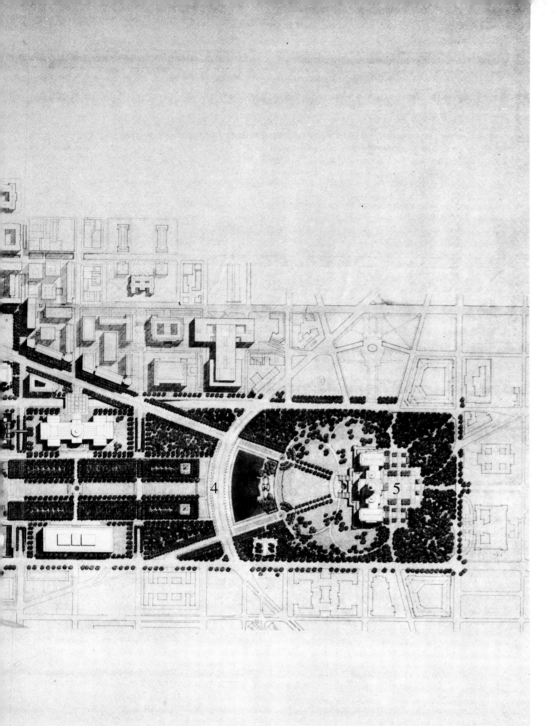

WASHINGTON MALL MASTER PLAN
INCLUDING THE PENNSYLVANIA AVENUE DEVELOPMENT

1 White House

2 National Square

3 Market Square

4 Capitol Reflecting Pool

5 New Capital Plaza with Underground Parking

6 Site of Hirshhorn Gallery—Major Cross Axis with National Sculpture Garden to North

7 Washington Monument Overlook and Visitor Center

8 West Potomac Park Recreation Area

9 Lincoln Memorial with New Restaurant and Visitor Facilities to northeast

10 New Termination for Reflecting Pool on 17th Street Axis. Rose Garden to northwest.

San Francisco overlooking Marin County.

Washington began as an idea that the most important monument to the republic should be established as a city.

Far different in its origins and growth has been a city that many have called the most beautiful in the world, and that might be described as the result of the evolution of a natural aesthetic—San Francisco.

I said earlier that to define an aesthetic was almost a hopeless challenge. In the ambience of San Francisco that challenge is met.

I have also said that one could reason an aesthetic out of existence. If we analyzed San Francisco's man-made additions to nature's endowment, we could end up with conclusive proof that she is the ugliest city in the world, not the most beautiful. She is endowed with what is probably the grandest array of natural physical assets any city ever had: a great Bay and fine harbor embraced by low foothills and fed by estuaries and the Sacramento River; a rich and fertile peninsula and mainland reminiscent of a small European country like Holland, Belgium or Luxembourg, with orchards, vineyards, dairy herds, villages, towns, fishing, shipping, recreation. And all of this is melded under the golden light of her complicated historical past, her mixture of races (from the Indian to the Mexican to the Russian, the Italian, the Chinese, the Japanese) and the culture left by the Franciscans in their mission churches along the coast.

Rather than a city or an "area," the Bay region of San Francisco is a frame of mind—a mental attitude—a place poised in a web of desire lines created through mobility. Her population of less than 800,000 has not affected her position as the so-called "Queen City of the West." She is the financial and business center in spite of the concentration of some 9 million-odd people in the metropolitan area of Los Angeles.

But even here, in this Eden of the West, there seem to be signs of a worm in the apple—Charles W. Moore, now Dean of the Yale School of Architecture but a long-time student of the San Francisco area, sounds a note of warning:

141

Since first the '49ers came through the Golden Gate and abandoned their ships along Montgomery Street, it has seemed as though the builders of San Francisco just couldn't miss; for over a century they have flung up row after row of some of the world's flimsiest and ugliest buildings in order to create one of the world's most beautiful cities; and on the occasions when the whole thing has fallen down (or burned up, as the inhabitants would prefer it), ignoring all sensible advice, they have with unprecedented slipshodness, built a more strange and wonderful city than ever. The fog helps, of course, and the bay, and some magic in the air. Daniel Burnham sought in vain to reform all this in the years before 1906, and nobody any more is particularly sorry that he failed; but watching the cage for John Graham's new Wells Fargo Bank rising up and out of touch with the city, it is hard to avoid wondering how soon Nob Hill (on its right) will go the way of Murray Hill, on Manhattan, vanished at the foot of skyscrapers. Will it be before the bad guys fill in the bay? For underneath the flimsies, it is the hills and the bay which develop the notion that San Francisco is a real city. It is certainly not, as it is in Chicago, for instance, the high-rise buildings which prove it. There is something different in the air in Chicago (the echo, perhaps, of Louis Sullivan) which gives power to high buildings there, be they round or square, or splayed like the old Monadnock buildings and the brand-new Brunswick Building. That power, and the control that goes with it, has never been in San Francisco. It is certainly not there now.

In large part, San Francisco has until recently answered the dictates of her geography—her waters and her hills—but from the beginning San Francisco has sturdily clamped her rigid grid of streets on her gently rolling foothills in direct disregard of the natural contours. Yet somehow she has managed to maintain the intellectual and cultural upper hand over Los Angeles with all her smog-enshrouded citizens.

A typical example of the San Franciscan's ability to snap back when confronted with adverse environmental intrusions concerns her attitude toward freeways, which, with the exception of Baltimore, are almost unique. Over ten years ago, the city was persuaded by the state of California that it needed an elevated freeway on its waterfront and was told that this freeway was absolutely essential; the fact that it blocked the view of the Ferry Building Campanile and destroyed the long vista of Market Street was unimportant. San Franciscans awoke to find that they had allowed one of the hallmarks of their traditions, the Embarcadero, to be obliterated. The slab is still there, but the public reaction was so strong that not one foot of freeway has been built since that date inside the city limits. It was an interesting case where the State Highway Commission won the battle and lost the war, since by building this short section of freeway, miles and miles of projected freeway remain unbuilt, blocked by public indignation. Someday the Embarcadero Freeway will probably be removed by an enlightened national policy adjusting to local demands, and Market Street can take her place with Pennsylvania Avenue, possibly one of the great boulevards in the world.

It is an intriguing fact that practically everyone the country over indicates a desire to live in San Francisco and yet the city itself is actually losing population. This is evidenced by the typical American concentration that is destroying rich orchard lands at an accelerated rate and converting them into a sea of faceless subdivisions. It is also evidenced by complete traffic tie-ups and hostility, creating a perpetual state of frustration over suburban living. But the spirit that guides San Francisco is clear, a type of common-sense approach that has resulted in the inauguration and financing of the first major regional rapid-transit system in the country. She has also launched one of the few successful urban renewal programs, in the form of the famous Golden Gateway project, which promises to draw back into the core city many thousands of people. There are efficient civic organizations at work controlling such vital matters as the sanctity of her Bay and her encircling, rolling hills. San Francisco is living proof that a true city is inextinguishable, that from the point of view of location, climate and desire lines crossing, man needs what such a core city offers—a place to trade, live, work, play and worship.

We have said that men and nations are known by what they serve. We have discussed carefully Chicago's Loop, Philadelphia's Center City, Washington's Mall and Pennsylvania Avenue and the unique enclave of San Francisco and her environments. Each offers evidence of a genuine effort toward urban renaissance, but why? What are we serving? What is our objective? Is it the city itself? Is it in the service of commercial growth; is it an effort toward self-preservation, or is it something on a grander scale? Is it not a search for an American aesthetic in the service of man reaching to fulfill his highest capacities? This renaissance is imperative in economic and practical terms, but it is even more so an act of great faith. Above all the material demands of our age, we know that the city serves as the best means by which man can know himself. The great challenge is to have the boldness to turn our urban liabilities into assets. There is neither profit nor honor in abandoning our cities to self-destruction, for they are the measure of our ability to be civilized. There we must take our stand.

San Francisco Embarcadero Freeway.

There is within us a need that cities cannot satisfy, however well they may be planned. As we have seen, there is something in our makeup that delights in open spaces. Increasingly, we gravitate toward city life, but we still succumb to the counterdraw of the open land.

As Freya Stark has reminded us, "beauty walks along the edge of opposites." There are lessons in our natural landforms as well as in our cities. We possess some of the most spectacular landscapes on earth, and the American aesthetic cannot but be affected by them, so long as we refrain from destroying them.

Far from the ramparts of our hundred-story buildings lie magnificent forms—a bend of a great river, a promontory encircled by the sea, the silhouette of a mountain range, the dry, sharp shadows of canyon lands, a swamp with winter-grayed stumps, warm, rolling hills—which have shaped much of our aesthetic consciousness. To have sampled such beauty is to love it forever.

I vividly recall, for example, the first acquaintance my wife and I made with the Olympic National Park in our Pacific Northwest, especially the rain forest threading up the slender valleys of Mount Olympus—the Hoh, the Quinault, the Queets and the Bogachiel—moist fingers down which clear rivers pour from the slopes of the mountain range.

As we entered the forest, my wife and I found ourselves under the perpetual fall of moisture which, combining with the mildness of the climate, has created a richness of lichen, oxalis, salal, sword fern, brachen and berry vines. Giant columns of Sitka spruce, hemlock, Douglas fir and red cedar reached 200 feet upward through floating shapes of big-leaf maple.

Like a living monument to the workings of change and continuity, the forest surrounded us with the signs of its centuries-long history. Embracing many of the trunks were growths of fungus which would in time bring the great trees down, leaving sky-lit windows in the forest roof. Through these openings would come sunshine and warmth so that the seedlings of future trees would take root and grow. Near already fallen trunks we could see new trees thriving, maintaining the continuing balance between life and death.

We entered the Bogachiel, crossing the river on horseback, moving with bowed heads among the branches, which closed behind us as if they had never been disturbed. We rode in a mysterious half-light which filtered through the columns. The sounds of life were a soft presence moving with us. The hush called up an infinity of time.

But the morning we returned along that trail, some two miles before we reached the Park boundary, we heard the nasal screaming of a mechanical saw on adjacent National Forest land. Time had suddenly become finite here. The Bogachiel Valley, with its ridge-line boundaries, so eloquent of the balance and continuity of life, was already being set off in its lower reaches by a steadily advancing graveyard of dead trees.

In such expanses of open land we will learn soon enough if we deserve the beauty and abundance of this land we have occupied. No longer desperate to clear our forests for homes or to conquer for the sake of conquering, we can afford to give the beauty of our land at least as much consideration as we do the "commodity value" of the trees we cut down and the ore we extract. The real test is in the question of whether we can see that an uncut forest or an unmined mountain has a higher value to society than the products resulting from their "use."

If we are to sustain a healthy balance of life in this country, we must preserve our natural resources, allowing animal and bird life as much right to exist as we do human life. To many this must seem like sentimentality. To those who have taken the effort to find out, it is clearly a matter of life and death *for all of us*. This is true not only biologically, but psychologically as well. Man needs enormous areas, unscarred by his own kind, as a primary source of spiritual recharging, and this need is as great as his requirement for material sustenance.

But to say this is not enough, for money talks louder and the claims of property drown out the claims of life. Private enterprise hears only what it wants to hear, and it listens for the promise of profit. Only national controls may be strong enough to curb their spendthrift policies.

In 1865, Joseph Henry and John Wesley Powell began such an effort against ignorance and greed. Their pioneering effort and the resulting establishment of the Smithsonian Institution, the National Geodetic Survey and the American Bureau of Ethnology have been indispensable to our growing understanding of what is at stake in preserving our natural assets, especially in the West. The next step must be the establishment of land banks and tree banks and a reversal of the trend of converting our rivers into irrigation canals with big dams in between.

Since the administration of Theodore Roosevelt we have had our national forests and our national parks. We have our Department of the Interior, with its cloudy, mismatched bureaus—the Bureau of Land Management, the Bureau of Indian Affairs, the Bureau of Reclamation—with only the

Aerial photograph of Mississippi River.

slender lance of the National Park Service opposing this
solid phalanx of poorly used power. The integrity of our
environment is under perpetual assault by money on the
make, and every congressman, senator and government employee is a potential area of vulnerability. The defenses that
matter are manned by special-interest groups whose main
strategy must be to arouse the conscience of the public. The
ability and success of this opposition varies with the "climate" of government policy and the relative awareness of
the usually apathetic private sector.

Surf and coast, Garapata Beach, Carmel,
California.

Humboldt Mountain Range, 30 miles east
of Elko, Nevada.

Pond in Connecticut.

The issues can be broken down as they affect three large subdivisions of territory. The first is made up of those areas already set aside and protected, but threatened anew. The Grand Canyon National Monument and the Colorado River await defacement by existing and proposed dams. The 59,000-acre rain forest, Olympic National Park, as we have seen, is under threat of being returned to the National Forest Service for cutting. Then there are areas which form a second category in possessing important scenic values and irreplaceable material resources which need federal protection before they are despoiled. The proposal for a National Redwood Park is an ideal example of this type of problem. Finally, there are those areas where existing agencies and procedures meant for land protection are being misused so that uses and rights permitted under the law are threatening to exhaust the natural resources. Many of our national forests and areas controlled by the Bureaus of Land Management and Reclamation are thus threatened. For example, in the great Cascades of the state of Washington, a virgin area proposed for a national park, mining claims for uranium and copper are permitted under the law to be worked, regardless of the damage. Similarly, on the Pacific Coast, there is a threat to locate oil refineries or atomic plants which would endanger the wildlife, resources and scenic beauty of great stretches of irreplaceable coastline.

All too little effort has been started to strengthen our defenses against the devastation. What has been started is dangerously undermined. It is a curious anomaly of our system that everyone who is out destroying our resources gets paid for doing it, while those who are trying to conserve our natural assets must do it on their own time, for free. Those in government who seek to preserve our resources are very often hindered by laws which can work against conservation.

What is most needed is an expert inventory of our national-resource problem, made by highly paid, efficient experts who can project with precision the benefits of conservation and the dangers of waste. Yet assessment of our environment and resources is the least organized and most poorly budgeted of our national requirements. Departments of environmental design are springing up all over the country, but they lack form and substance. The Bureau of Reclamation is turning out to be the wrecker of its sister bureau, the valuable National Park Service. And since there are few voters living on the enormous areas under attack, the high-powered commercial lobbies face little opposition from the indigenous population.

Few people may live in our open lands, but *there* is where our national substance lies. Our rivers, mountains, forests, and shorelines—our grasslands and deserts—preceded us. Their majesty influenced our national spirit. Their beauty offers us rest and inspiration. We accept them as our birthright, while the interests of commerce assume the right to destroy them.

STRUCTURES IN PLACE

Architecture has many faces. It has been called the printing press of all ages, for it leaves in its structures a description of the society in which it works. Architecture has also been called essentially a social art, and it has been said of modern architecture that it should organize the forces of modern society, discipline them for humane ends and express them through the utilitarian and plastic forms of buildings.

Great architects have offered challenging concepts expressing what the key to design should be. Louis Henry Sullivan provoked a revolution in design by maintaining that form is function and that utility cannot be the stepchild of the builder's art. Frank Lloyd Wright turned to the impress of nature for his inspiration, arguing that buildings should be organic; that is, at one with their surroundings and their purpose. Le Corbusier emphasized another form of modernity with his call for "a machine for living," while Miës van der Rohe has insisted on discipline and control—in his formula, "Less is more."

These architects, and many like them, have responded to the vast changes of our times. New materials, new methods of construction and new needs on the part of society have dynamically broadened the prospects of architecture. In our cities, great new buildings reflect the activity, the enterprise and the change that mark the urban environment.

There is another major aspect to architecture—another face—molded not by a world of mechanisms but by the land itself. The terrain in its varied forms also inspires, and even dictates to, the perceptive architect natural forms for his structures. Confronted with surrounding hills or mountains or plains, that builder who would impose a man-made form upon nature strives to design works that seem to rise out of the ground into the sun. Architecture can be a kind of oratory of power—by means of form.

There are probably no original forms still undiscovered, and few left to be invented, and so architecture will look to the complex of images we have already created, to the many forms and concepts we know and to the land itself to be the variables that will make new ideas possible.

It is not a problem to create monumental buildings. Sheer size is no longer a legitimate source of pride. The real challenge is how to integrate individual buildings into the larger design of our communities. We must judge our cities as totalities where the whole is greater than the sum of the parts. Architecture is the art of meaningful forms in space, each form gaining significance from the context of those surrounding it. In that totality, our buildings are words bespeaking our aesthetic, our skylines are like sentences, our building complexes are like paragraphs; and they reflect

Monument Valley, Arizona, looking north into Utah.

style and taste, or the lack of them.

Because our aesthetic style is embodied in how we live, the structures it produces should be the kind that individuals can live, work, play, worship and celebrate in as men, not machines. Today, in shaping our physical environment, we tend toward orderly solutions of precision, measurement and logic. The great leveling influences of mass-production items are tending toward a society of conformity. The antidote to this is style—distinctive, original, architectural wit, avoidance of monotony.

The structures pictured in this chapter have been placed either in man-made or natural environments so as to complement their settings. They need no word descriptions to reveal their style—the reader's eye and acumen are sufficient. If a building or bridge or statue cannot speak for itself, there is nothing important to be said for it.

Glen Canyon Dam and Bridge, Page, Arizona.

Central Park, New York City. [Lee Boltin]

Pueblo San Felipe, New Mexico. Note
the large area devoted to the public square.

Carson Pirie Scott, Chicago. Louis Sullivan, Architect. [From *The Idea of Louis Sullivan* by John Szarkowski, © copyright 1956 by the University of Minnesota.]

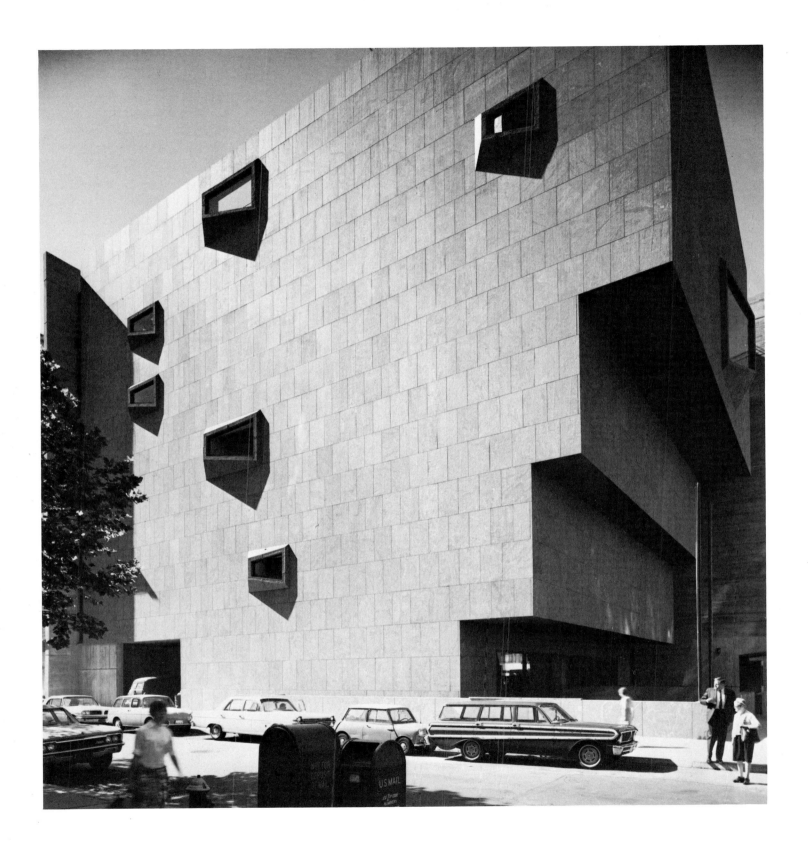

Whitney Museum of American Art. Marcel
Breuer and Hamilton Smith, Architects.
[© Ezra Stoller (ESTO)]

Whitney—detail of overhang.

Whitney—entrance and sculpture court.

Dulles International Airport, Washington, D.C. Eero Saarinen Associates, Architects. [J. Warigg Stinchcomb]

Dulles International Airport, Washington, D.C. [Balthazar Korab]

Oakland-Alameda County Coliseum, Oakland, California. Skidmore, Owings & Merrill, Architects/Engineers. [© Ezra Stoller (ESTO)]

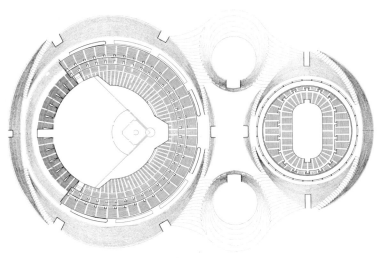

Contour plan, baseball.

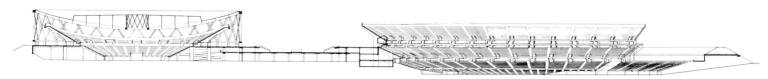

Cross section through arena (above), plaza (exhibit space under plaza) and stadium.

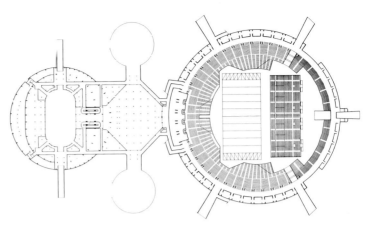

Concourse plan—football.

Mauna Kea Beach Hotel, Kamuela, Hawaii. Skidmore, Owings & Merrill, Architects/Engineers. [R. Wenkam]

Alcoa Building, San Francisco, California.
Skidmore, Owings & Merrill, Architects/
Engineers.

[Morley Baer]

Air Force Academy Chapel, Colorado
Springs, Colorado. Skidmore, Owings &
Merrill, Architects/Engineers.

[Stewart's]

[Laura Gilpin]

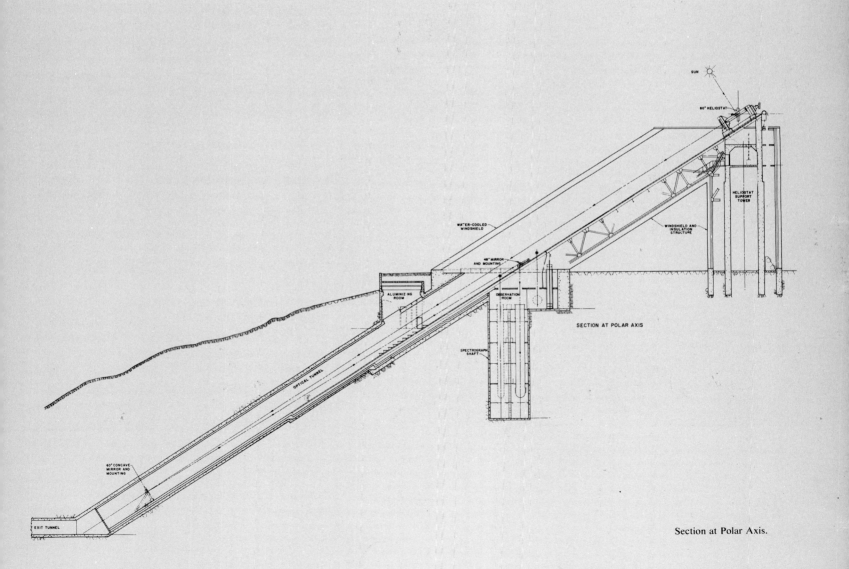

SUN

90" HELIOSTAT

HELIOSTAT
SUPPORT
TOWER

WATER-COOLED
WINDSHIELD

WINDSHIELD AND
INSULATION
STRUCTURE

48" MIRROR
AND MOUNTING

ALUMINIZING
ROOM

OBSERVATION
ROOM

SECTION AT POLAR AXIS

SPECTROGRAPH
SHAFT

OPTICAL TUNNEL

60" CONCAVE
MIRROR AND
MOUNTING

EXIT TUNNEL

Section at Polar Axis.

Civic Center for Marin County, California.
Frank Lloyd Wright, Architect.

[Dandelet]

Chicago Circle Campus, University of Illinois. Skidmore, Owings & Merrill, Architects/Engineers.

[Ben Denison Studio]

St. John's Abbey Church, Collegeville,
Minnesota. Marcel Breuer and Hamilton
Smith, Architects.

[Shin Koyama]

The Joseph H. Hirshhorn Museum and Sculpture Garden and National Sculpture Garden, Washington, D.C. Skidmore, Owings & Merrill, Architects/Engineers.

[Dwain Faubion]

Elevation looking south (cross section through Hirshhorn Sculpture Garden).

Pablo Picasso sculpture, Chicago Civic Center, Chicago, Illinois.

EPILOGUE

In the works of design and construction just reviewed, two qualities seem to stand out as tokens of promise. One is the continuing search for new aesthetic expression, in a contemporary idiom. The second is youthfulness. However old these structures may be, they embody a youthful spirit which has always been a prime ingredient in great design.

Idealism and youthful innovation similarly have been vital in our nation's development. The present swift rise in the proportion of young people to the total population marks youth as our prime natural resource and concern. What future have we to offer this reservoir of energy? Our average young American adult is a debt-ridden man, whose house, probably located in a new tract development, is mortgaged and burdened with "special assessments" from a regiment of conflicting taxing bodies, each trying to find ways of paying the costs of new schools, fire and police departments, sewage systems and other utilities. His house is filled with costly electrical labor-saving devices advertised in the mass media and his garage contains at least one car. These mainstays of the economy have been financed through long-term payment plans including financing rates averaging one-twelfth of the cost of the products. Considered so essential for domestic ease, the monthly payments for these conveniences may well force his wife to work to make ends meet; and this in turn increases the burden as she finds a second car indispensable for her job. Meanwhile, the national inflation spiral accelerates.

External pressures require participation in civic affairs: evening meetings over threats to the neighborhood by intruding freeways; threats to the single-family dwelling by permissive zoning for high-rise apartments, industrial complexes, commercial elements, motels and gas stations, with their attendant signs and wires; and the increase of air and water pollution. The beleaguered family is bombarded by piecemeal and contradictory proposals from the town council or board of supervisors for projects that are allegedly designed to "improve" the community and that are often brilliantly presented by developers. Planning and architectural advice to guide our citizen in his actual best interests is virtually nonexistent. In fact, the local professional talent is often dependent for commissions on the very sources that are planning the destruction of the neighborhood.

Routinely, the day is launched for the citizen in his two-car garage. He climbs into his new-model automobile, which is financed by an agency provided by the manufacturer, and, after breathing deadly exhaust fumes when the traffic clogs, finally arrives at his place of employment. Behind his desk he shuffles papers or pushes buttons. If he happens to be a

Aerial photograph of ice patterns, Mormon Lake, Arizona.

young executive, the routine office procedures of the in-depth corporate structure involve him in innumerable telephone calls, interspersed with interminable meetings and conferences.

His boss, a senior executive, has himself been deprived of opportunities for creative work by the conventions of the system under which our corporate entities exist. Legal questions are funneled to legal specialists. Federal and state commissions and agencies control his attempts to innovate. Of special concern to the board of directors and to the management is the corporation's public image; this, too, is formed and directed by outside specialists in public relations and the mass media. Our executive seldom participates even in the writing of his own speeches. He is a channeled entity in his own organization.

The public is encouraged to buy shares of the company's stock which are bought and sold by and for people who know or care little about the actual integrity of the product. Such an environment and such a series of restrictions automatically make our executive feel less than inspired.

Norbert Weiner, in *The Human Use of Human Beings* makes the awesome prediction that much of the work being done by millions of wage-earners today will rapidly be taken over by automatically operated machines. What geometric repeat patterns will be formulated when entire areas of employment, workers in stores, offices and factories—the human element—are phased out of existence? Weiner believes that what the machine can do, the machine should do. Yet we must ask, in what new direction can these displaced job holders turn? How will we engage the creative energies of the vast number of young people who are facing the problem of an automated society? Is it surprising that there is discontent among them? In fact, we should be even more apprehensive if our intelligent and often talented youth were not concerned over the prospects of wasting their energy, enthusiasm and spirit in a world which offers little in return but the possibility of monetary security. It is encouraging that many of them are vocal about their doubts and ask embarrassing questions as to the meaning of our society. But our answers lack depth and understanding as we hand them this world we have made, saying "Fit into the pattern and make something of it!" And as they consider what we offer, is it unreasonable that they ask, "Why conform to a pattern we don't like?"

Some of us are shocked and wonder what has brought about this change in young people. Yet have they changed? The grandson of the man who plowed with a team of Clydesdales down on the farm in Indiana programs a computer.

He's an electrical engineer, but I doubt very much that there is any great difference between him and his forebears. His view may be broader in a scientific environment but he carries roots of logic from his forebears. With his talent and with the tools of our modern society at hand he and thousands of others like him—including those who have temporarily "dropped out"—can plan, develop and conduct intricate logistical operations that provide the needs of our society. It would seem that this is being done miraculously for there is no written law or master plan to guide the actions of the myriad individual agencies involved. Yet, at any given point on a three-quarter-acre portion of Wall Street, in any 40-, 50- or 60-story building, some 15,000 people can demand and get satisfaction for their needs as a result of this loosely handled, worldwide system of logistical support. The talent that accomplishes this miraculous task is the progeny of that which guided the Roman conquerors who administered the *pax Romana* without any of the equipment available to us today. And can't we trace a similar lineage of genius back to the inspiration of the cathedral builders of the twelfth and thirteenth centuries who conceived and created the cathedral of Chartres and its rose window?

Such capacity for marshaling ideas, men and resources is not as rare as we may at first suppose. Its supply depends on demand. We must give our young men opportunities to try their innovations. There is an unlimited variety of systems and devices designed to do the mechanical job of carrying out theoretical explorations, provided there is a basic idea with which to work. The fulcrum needed for this leverage of opportunity is our democratic system of government and free enterprise. The existing environment is sufficiently intact to be salvageable. Our high-density population centers can be reorganized and rebuilt on less area than they now occupy and the resulting open spaces can be rededicated for recreation and aesthetic purposes. Density tolerances which will allow for the predicted growth in population can be developed, as illustrated by the Chicago Loop plan. From our present chaos can come ordered open and urban spaces—an order into which a new comprehension of man's ecology and nature's ecology must be introduced. The first step required to set this program in motion involves a firm commitment to subordinate our disposable product economy to an all-out capital investment commitment for improving and protecting the function and beauty of our *permanent* environment.

If size, volume and dollar value were the only criteria, it would not be hard to prove that we are capable of such an effort, considering the enormous public and private projects in evidence on all sides today. Our capabilities appear to be unlimited when individual projects are involved. We are able to develop virtually unlimited markets and to produce products for them. Unfortunately, however, we have not found the key to redirecting that power. Obscured by myth, superstition, apathy and greed, the way eludes us.

Nevertheless, there are certain signs of a changing, hopeful climate, as indicated by youthful protest and new attitudes of elected and appointed officials of government. Another sign of hope is evidence of better understanding of the problems of water and soil conservation. That we are considering these in the light of ecological boundaries rather than arbitrary political lines is encouraging. Nevertheless, there is still a long way to go. The Department of the Interior, supported by an impressive body of statutory laws, is vested through the secretary and the bureau chiefs with enormous power, but no administrative branch of government is free to move beyond or against the will of the concerned congressional committees from which their power stems. To date such power is directed by commercial pressure lobbies. Meanwhile the conservation forces, because of internal schisms, have failed to develop their own power potential.

The task force necessary to accomplish this proposed renaissance must be recruited in part from those about to be phased out of jobs through automation. In addition to this, it is interesting to think of what might happen if those millions presently working on defense, highway programs and the space industry were suddenly made available. And, of course, the largest and most important area of enlistment may be the uncommitted youth now under twenty-five years of age (approximately one-half the population).

I do not wish to speak lightly of the jobless but I suggest looking at them in a new light. They should be looked at as a potential. Job-free, they may be directed by creative, imaginative leaders to direct their energies to discover ways of making beauty and well-being available to all. These energies could be harnessed to rebuilding our cities. And where the mechanical advantages in science and industry could be used to implement their efforts, a magnificent era could occur; where the wisdom of conservationists prevailed, vast regions could be planted with trees, erosion halted and the destruction caused by man repaired. An upheaval, positive in nature, with new starting points and new definitions of terms is required, with revolutionary ideas turning work into play and abandoning the national goal of production for profit, replacing it with a drive for restoring a satisfactory environment. We already have many things

going for us. Each great civilization has built and rebuilt its cities, from the Euphrates to the Nile to the Greek Isles to Imperial Rome. The ability to conceive and design and execute total environments has been demonstrated. If we are a great civilization we can do the same for our country.

What kind of education, training, leadership is needed to produce the blueprint for such a dream? It will not come from conventional sources. Contemporary city planners, architects and engineers are products of conceptual systems we know have failed. Not that the professions are inoperative—quite the contrary. The modern corporate executive usually chooses an architect known for an individual trademark, such as a grill or arch, much as he might choose for sculpture a Henry Moore or a Giocametti. In this way a premium is put upon the packaging rather than the plan and function, and the goal is to fit a startling shape over a piece of utilitarian space. This system makes no provision for controlling the environment of this masterpiece against future adverse intrusions. The "name" architects who handle this kind of product design are few in number and tend to exert about the same influence on the profession as a whole as the wedding cake on the baking industry. This practice of purchasing product design is in itself not objectionable, except that the attention given it tends to obscure the real contribution that the profession makes to the total environment.

The problems of environmental control in broad depth should be our profession's greatest concern. Although our cities are studded with highly visible, much publicized individual constructions, the thirty thousand or more registered architects have little or nothing to do with these and are occupied with far less colorful commissions. They become basically craftsmen, performing the utilitarian functions required by the everyday life of our towns, cities and megalopolises. These practitioners have the bread and butter work to do, the unglamorous jobs of producing schools, for instance, within budgets that are too low, on predetermined sites located in the wrong areas for populations that are growing and changing too fast too soon. Theirs is a constant struggle to earn a living without compromising their aesthetic or ethical standards, to serve on civic boards and commissions, contributing special knowledge without which the community is at the mercy of the speculator. Like the medical corps on the field of battle they try to staunch environmental wounds as best they can and to stem forces that they had no hand in releasing and little power to control.

In a similar context there are the engineers with whom the architect engages in continuous conflict, blaming all manner of sins upon them. The fact is that much of what the engineer does for the architect is creative and indispensable. His service to the architect involves making even the more tortured of architectural designs stand. But the engineering profession has a life of its own and in the field of design, and often construction, handles about ninety percent of the type of installations or constructions that literally change the face of the land. The engineer creates heroic images in the form of huge dams, reservoirs and irrigation works. He designs and builds huge chemical complexes, harbors, docks, shipyards, the nation's sewage and water treatment plants. He has laced a network of pipelines and highways across the continent. He is the principal instrument through which the face of our continent has been altered, but he is the implementor rather than the creator of broad policies and master ideas Thus in engineering design the vital aesthetic ingredient is often missing. Yet when the talents of both professions, architectural and engineering, are properly joined, great works of utility and aesthetic beauty can result.

But if we cannot look to the architect and the engineer for guidance, then where can we look? Who will provide the blueprint? History shows that the great leaders of men were seldom professionals. The Pharaohs, the Caesars, the great Popes, for example, conceived and directed the building of much magnificence. Haussmann and Napoleon III rebuilt Paris. Washington and Jefferson provided the imagination and courage to design our capital city. All evidence seems to point toward the statesman-politician, aided by some form of urban concept team, as the source of leadership to implement the programs of a government and private sector, to join together, forming a conservation, environment-oriented working party.

Guidelines for such a program, designed for the creation of the machinery for developing a better environment would include:

Choice of Profession: A variety of professions and disciplines are relevant since every facet of education has an application to the subject. But let there be a strong desire for thoroughness and mastery embodied in the choice. Let it be certain that those selected for training have the capabilities to absorb the knowledge and assume the power necessary to do the job. The role of government, and the appropriate curricula for the proper preparation of those who intend to enter it as a career, must be defined and implemented. The science of government should be given the dignity of an established profession. Although governmental involvement with our environment is basic, and although a form of socialism in this country already exists, the private

sector under such joint efforts as those proposed by the "urban coalition" could out-perform and be far superior to any type of government bureaucracy. Young people must look at the balance sheet and note the difference between the short-range gains of our profit system and the long-range costs of dissipation of natural resources in repairing the blight, poverty and distress this system often causes.

A Question of Land Tenure: Our system of land tenure is inherited from an earlier agrarian society and is a cornerstone of our total land-use structure. At the root of our private enterprise lies this system which respects the right of the landowner to use and misuse his own property, regardless of the effect of that action on the public interest. Whether a basic questioning of the rights, privileges and practices of our private enterprise system calls for the nationalization of our natural resources is the cause of sharp disagreement, with bitterness and passion replacing reasonable debate. Unresolved confrontations exist today in most areas of the country. Examples include the Hudson River case involving New York's Consolidated Edison and the Storm King Highway; the steel industry versus preservation of the Indiana dunes; the pollution of Lake Tahoe; the Redwood National Park controversy involving private timber interests, the Sierra Club, Save-The-Redwoods League versus the State of California and the federal government; the defense of San Francisco Bay against attempts to fill in its perimeter. This last case offers an example where both points of view have a solid basis for a last-stand defense of their positions. Those who own the land, such as the salt flats under water, might appear to have a legal right to fill it. Those who defend the integrity of the existing shoreline can prove that the Bay is the most important physical asset for the well-being of the total region and that to lose it would destroy the economic structure as well as undermine the health and welfare of its population.

A corollary to the problem of curtailing private property rights in the public interest is the root question of the economic impact on the efforts of private enterprise to exploit a natural resource, and, in the process, to destroy the environment. Is not the long-term impact of the economic welfare of a given area immeasurably better when restraint and foresight are practiced with its resources rather than the short-term conversion of the resource into inflation-inclined dollars? Doesn't the simplest accounting clearly show that the destroyed environment, plundered of its natural resources, becomes a public liability and its population a public charge?

A Natural Resources Bank: Based on an exhaustive study, an inventory of ecological regions incorporating quantitative and qualitative interrelationships of every type of land, body of water, mineral, flora and fauna should be established. To augment this, Congress should authorize a national resources bureau under the executive branch of the federal government and endow it with the type of authority and prestige enjoyed by the Bureau of the Budget. It would be the function of this bureau to protect and control the disposition and use of the natural resources encompassed under the authority of the national resources bank.

On an isolated bank of the Nile, the great temple of Abu Simbel was carved from living rock some three thousand years ago. Recent flooding from the Aswan Dam would have submerged its magnificent colossal statues if the temple had not been moved to a higher site by an international team of engineers, archaeologists and architects. Expensive though the task has been, the temple itself is priceless, even though it was dedicated to a now dead religion, is without any present practical function and certainly provides no return in capital gain. In addition, its isolation will only allow it to be viewed by comparatively few people. In spite of this "uselessness," it was moved with the skill, care and precision of a surgical operation, by Swedes, Italians, Germans and Americans, an undertaking costing over thirty million dollars. The funds for this operation were raised through an international subscription.

Such an act of faith in the rightness of beauty as a supreme motivating power, such enthusiasm for value beyond the here and now, such willingness to come together and to contribute talent and energy without concern for immediate profit—these are precisely the spurs to cooperative action and inspired "play" that we should offer our youth.

No particular discipline or group of disciplines is exclusively superior for the work at hand. All of our knowledge and functions have gone into making the environment what it is today, good and bad. The same totality can change it. Some areas of study and effort, especially those having to do with ecology, deserve a higher priority, but the student who develops a high sense of literary style or an expertise in philosophy or a solid grounding in economics and history, a training in the arts or a knowledge of the natural sciences, can effectively help in bringing about this change, just as can the anthropologist, the chemist or the transportation specialist. We can offer them plenty of action.

In his faith in himself and something greater than himself, man has been capable of beautiful works, massive and delicate. In our time it appears that man has again reached for the wrong fruit and is heading for a second Fall, this time

Irrigated orchard, Sacramento Valley, California.

193

from the splendor of his own humanity. If that is the way he is heading, he must produce a miracle that will turn him toward a rebirth of that splendor.

If we can come together to free ourselves for a world in which there will be room not only for vibrant cities but also for rolling hills, dense green forests and bright seas beyond; and if, at peace with ourselves and each other, we can savor the substances of nature as wonders and not spoils of combat, then that miracle will occur and the life-giving aesthetic be realized.

General Grant Tree.

INDEX

NATHANIEL ALEXANDER OWINGS

One of America's most distinguished architects and planners, Nathaniel Alexander Owings was born in Indianapolis in 1903. He attended the University of Illinois and received his bachelor's degree in architecture from Cornell University in 1927.

With Louis Skidmore, he founded Skidmore, Owings & Merrill, in 1936. Among the many projects this major architectural firm has completed under Mr. Owings' direction are the Lever Brothers and Chase Manhattan buildings in New York, the Crown Zellerbach and Alcoa buildings in San Francisco, the John Hancock building in Chicago, the Oakland, California, Coliseum and the Qantas Hotel in Sydney, Australia.

First appointed by President John F. Kennedy, Mr. Owings has served as Chairman of the Council for the Redesign of Pennsylvania Avenue and of President Johnson's Temporary Commission on Pennsylvania Avenue. He was Chairman of the Chicago Planning Commission for nearly four years and is a member of the National Advisory Board to the Secretary of the Interior on National Parks, Historic Sites, Buildings and Monuments. He is a trustee of the American Academy in Rome, a Fellow of the American Institute of Architects and a member of the National Academy of Art.

Mr. Owings lives in Big Sur, California, with his wife, Margaret.

WILLIAM A. GARNETT

America's foremost aerial photographer, William A. Garnett has pioneered many important photographic techniques since World War II. A native of California, he has flown more than 700,000 miles photographing all sections of the country for foundations, magazine and book publishers, corporations and various agencies.

His work has been included in over one hundred group exhibitions in museums and universities around the world, and has been shown in eight exhibitions by the Museum of Modern Art in New York. Among the many publications that have featured his photography are *Holiday*, *Time*, *Sports Illustrated*, *The Saturday Review*, *Look*, *American Heritage*, *U.S. Camera*, *Harper's*, *Horizon* and *Architectural Forum*.

Mr. Garnett was the first aerial photographer to be awarded a Guggenheim Fellowship. He is currently a research fellow for the Foundation for Environmental Design and is photographing the coastal area of California to document land use and its relationships to open space. He is also a fellow of the Center for Advanced Visual Studies at the Massachusetts Institute of Technology and is Chairman of the Department of Visual Arts at the University of California at Berkeley.

He makes his home in Napa, California.